GW00418134

Translator: Andrew Pastwood

This edition first published in 1993 by
Sunburst Books, Deacon House, 65 Old Church Street,
London, SW3 5BS

Copyright © Editorial LIBSA, Narciso Serra, 25 – Tel 433 54 07 –
28007 MADRID
4.ª EDICION 1991
Copyright English language text © 1993 Sunburst Books

All rights reserved. No part of this publication may be reproduced,
stored in a retrieval system, or transmitted in any form or by any
means, electronic, mechanical, photocopying, recording, or otherwise,
without the prior written permission of the Publisher.

ISBN 1 85778 009 4

Printed and bound in China

EXOTIC ORIENTAL COOKING

CONTENTS

INTRODUCTION

The cuisine of the Far East is made up of a myriad of exotic flavours and seasonings, most of which are unfamiliar to western palates. This abundance of different tastes and the wide variety of culinary techniques used throughout the Far East have evolved as a result of centuries of intermingled cultures and customs in the region.

Chinese cuisine, which varies tremendously from the most basic dishes to highly sophisticated preparations, is probably the most well-known outside Asia. The Chinese influence is also the most widespread throughout the entire Far Eastern region, particularly in Thailand, Burma, Vietnam, Malaysia and Indonesia. Indian cookery has also played a key role in shaping the cuisine of these countries.

Although the cuisines of the eight countries presented in this book are quite distinctive, there is one important common element which binds them all together - rice. Rice is the focal point of every meal, although the preference for certain types of rice varies from region to region. The Chinese prefer a long-grain variety, while the more glutinous, short-grain type predominates in Malaysia and Indonesia.

Another feature common to the cuisine of many Asian countries is that it is subject to rigid religious restrictions. Food consumption, and particularly the consumption of meat products, is dictated in many countries by either Hinduism, Buddhism or Islam. Hindus are not allowed to eat beef, Muslims must avoid pork and Buddhists place great symbolic significance on the methods of cooking and presenting their meals.

This book provides the reader with a regional overview of Asian cuisine and with the practical resources required to try out many of the most popular and delicious recipes from the Far East.

To facilitate this, the first chapter presents a glossary of spices and condiments, and the methods of preparing them for use in various dishes. Asterisks have been included in the ingredients lists of the recipes throughout the book to indicate those preparations which can be found in the first chapter.

CONDIMENTS AND SPICES

FENUGREEK

This is from the Mediterranean region, but is also grown in India. The seeds are used as a spice.

BUTTERMILK

This is a low fat milk made with a culture.

BURMESE BALACHAN

20 garlic cloves, chopped
4 onions, peeled and chopped
500 ml/18 fl oz peanut oil
250 g/9 oz dried shrimp powder
2 tsp cayenne
2 tsp salt
1 tsp dried shrimp paste
100 ml/3¹/₂ fl oz wine vinegar

Fry the garlic and onions in the oil until golden. Remove from the pan, drain well and combine with the remaining ingredients. Store in the refrigerator.

CARDAMOM

This is a herbaceous plant, native to India and Ceylon. The seeds have a delicate flavour and are used in curries and sweets.

TURMERIC

It is the rhizome, or rootlike stem of this plant that is used, almost always in powdered form. It is used mainly as colouring, since it gives a strong yellow colour to foods.

MINT CHUTNEY

30 g/1 oz fresh mint leaves, finely chopped
6 spring onions, coarsely chopped
2 fresh green peppers, seeded and chopped
1 garlic clove, chopped
1 tsp salt
2 tsp sugar
1 tsp garam masala
75 ml/2¹/₂ fl oz lemon juice
1 tbsp water

Place some of the chopped mint leaves, spring onions, peppers and garlic in a mortar and pound with a pestle to achieve a paste. Continue adding small quantities of the mint, onions, peppers and garlic, and pounding until they are all used up. Mix in the remaining ingredients and keep in a jar in the refrigerator.

DAUN PANDAN

Daun pandan is the leaves of the pandanus (Pandanus latifolia) which is used to add flavour to rice and curries. It is also used in sweets and pastries in Malaysia and Indonesia. The wide, flat leaves are boiled and chopped to add flavouring and green colouring to dishes.

TRANSPARENT NOODLES

These noodles are made out of the starch from a variety of beans called mung beans (Phaselos radiatus). Depending on how they are to be used, they can be soaked in hot water, boiled or fried. Transparent noodles are used as a side dish and may be bought in speciality shops.

GALINGALE

This is a large herbaceous plant from Thailand and southern China. The rhizome, or root, is used to give a cool, fresh flavour.

GARAM MASALA

There are several variations of this mixture of spices, and as long as the ingredients used are of good quality, it will keep for quite a long time if stored in an airtight container. Here is one of the most commonly used recipes for garam masala.

3 tbsp coriander seeds
4 tsp cumin seeds
2 tsp black peppercorns
4 tsp cardamom pods
4 sticks cinnamon 7.5 cm/3 inches long
1 tsp cloves
1 whole nutmeg

Heat the coriander, cumin, peppercorns, cardamom, cinnamon and cloves separately in a dry frying-pan. When each spice begins to give off its aroma, turn on to a plate and leave to cool.

Remove the cardamom seeds from the pods, grate the nutmeg, grind all the spices together and keep in an airtight jar.

Top: Dried Shrimp Paste
Bottom: Coconut Milk

particles. Allow to cool at room temperature, then chill until the butter solidifies. Remove the fat from the surface with a spoon and leave the residue. Heat the fat again and pour through a muslin-lined sieve to rid it of any remaining solid particles. Ghee keeps for 3-4 months without refrigeration.

CURRY LEAVES

These are the leaves from an Asian tree called the Murraya koeningii, which belongs to the citrus fruit tree family. It grows in abundance in certain regions of Asia. The leaves are usually used fresh and are fried in oil to make them crunchy before making the curry. They may also be ground into powdered form.

COCONUT MILK AND CREAM

The clear liquid that is found in the middle of coconuts is usually known as coconut milk. However, true coconut milk comes from the grated flesh of a ripe,

GHEE

This is purified butter made by heating the butter in a pan until it becomes frothy. The froth on the surface is removed with a spoon and the hot butter is poured into a heatproof bowl, leaving behind the solid

Left: Red Curry Powder
Centre: Curry Leaves
Right: Madras Curry Powder

fresh coconut. This is very easy to make.

For about 225 ml/8 fl oz coconut milk, place 90 g/3 oz grated fresh coconut in a food processor or liquidizer. Add 225 ml/8 fl oz hot water and blend for 5 minutes. Allow to cool for 30 minutes then strain through thick muslin or cheesecloth, pressing to extract as much liquid as possible. Pour into a clear measuring jug and leave for another 30 minutes. The coconut cream will rise to the top of the milk and can be spooned off for use
as required.

Coconut milk is also available in cans from specialist stores, it is much richer than home-made milk. Coconut cream is sold in packages the size of a block of butter. To use, follow the instructions on the packet.

CANDLENUT

This is a very hard nut from the tropical Aleuritis moluccana tree. It is used frequently in Indonesia and Malaysia to add flavour to curries. It may be replaced by Brazil nuts (Bertholletia excelsa),

although Brazils have a less pronounced flavour and are less sweet.

DRIED SHRIMP PASTE

This has a very strong flavour and is sold in specialist shops in cans or jars. It keeps indefinitely without refrigeration. If unavailable, anchovy paste may be used instead.

MADRAS CURRY PASTE

160 g/6 oz ground coriander
90 g/3 oz ground cumin
2 tsp ground black pepper
2 tsp ground turmeric
2 tsp ground black mustard seeds
2 tsp cayenne
2 tsp salt
2 garlic cloves, peeled and crushed
2 tsp ginger root, crushed
wine vinegar to bind the mixture, as needed
170 ml/6 fl oz vegetable oil

Combine the dry spices with the salt in a mixing bowl. Add the garlic, the ginger

and a little vinegar to obtain a smooth, thick purée.

Heat the oil in a pan and when very hot add the spice mixture. Turn down the heat and stir constantly until the spices are cooked and the oil begins to separate from them. Allow to cool then store in a jar.

Two teaspoons of this paste is normally used for each 500 g/1 lb 2 oz of meat, poultry or fish. It replaces the garlic, ginger and other spices that are normally used in a curry.

RED THAI CURRY PASTE

4 dried red chilis
2 small onions, peeled and chopped
1 tsp black peppercorns
1 tsp ground cumin
1 tsp ground coriander
2 tsp coriander seeds
1 tsp salt
1 tsp grated lemon rind
1 tsp chopped lemon balm
1 tsp ground galingale

2 tsp paprika
1 tsp ground turmeric
1 garlic clove, chopped
2 tsp dried shrimp paste
1 tsp vegetable oil

Remove the stalks from the chilis, but do not remove the seeds, since they add flavour to this very strong Thai curry paste. Blend the chilis with the other ingredients in a food processor or blender until a paste is obtained. To bind the

Left: Green Curry Powder
Right: Garam Masala

mixture well, it is advisable to add 2 teaspoons of oil or water.

GREEN THAI CURRY PASTE

4 large green chilis
1 tsp green peppercorns
1 small onion, peeled and chopped
1 garlic clove, chopped
4 tsp chopped fresh coriander
2 tsp chopped lemon rind
1 tsp salt
2 tsp ground coriander
1 tsp ground coriander
1 tsp ground cumin
1 tsp ground balm
1 tsp ground galingale
2 tsp dried shrimp paste
1 tsp ground turmeric
2 tsp vegetable oil

Remove the stalks from the chilis, but do not remove the seeds if a very strong curry is desired. Place in a food processor or blender with the remaining ingredients and blend until a purée is obtained. To prevent the mixture sticking to the sides of the blender scrape the mixture off from time to time. Add a little more oil, if necessary, to bind the mixture effectively.

BURMESE DRIED SHRIMP POWDER

Lightly toast 120 g/4 oz dried shrimps in a dry frying-pan. Using a pestle and mortar mash them until they have turned to powder. In the same pan, fry the shrimp powder in a little oil for about 5 minutes, then add a pinch of paprika and salt and a dash of vinegar. Fry until the mixture becomes crunchy. Leave to cool, add 1 tablespoon fried, finely chopped onions and garlic and keep in a jar.

BASIC RECIPE FOR AN INDONESIAN SAMBALAN

15 dried red chilis
3 onions, peeled and chopped
8 garlic cloves, peeled
2 tsp dried shrimp paste
100 ml/3¹/₂ fl oz peanut oil
225 ml/8 fl oz tamarind liquid
3 tsp salt
pepper
2 tbsp brown sugar

Soak the chilis in hot water for 10 minutes. Drain and place in a food processor or blender with the onions, garlic and shrimp paste and blend with enough of the oil to make a paste.
Heat the remaining oil in a frying-pan and sauté the chili paste, stirring constantly until it looks cooked and the oil begins to

separate from the paste. Rinse the blender with the tamarind liquid and pour into the frying-pan. Season with salt and pepper, add the brown sugar and cook for a few minutes, stirring constantly. Leave to cool and keep in a jar in the refrigerator.
To use, heat the desired amount (approximately 2 tsp for every 250 g/9 oz of the main ingredient in the dish) and combine it with the main ingredient before cooking.

ONION SAMBAL

4 tsp lemon juice
¹/₂ tsp cayenne
¹/₂ tsp salt
2 medium onions, peeled and chopped

Sprinkle the lemon juice, cayenne and salt over the chopped onion and mix well.
This is used as a relish to accompany curries and lamb dishes.

INDONESIAN SAMBAL-ULEK

25 red chilis
wine vinegar or tamarind liquid, as needed
2 tsp salt

This is a chili paste used in many Indonesian dishes. To make it, place the whole chilis in a blender or food processor. Blend with enough vinegar or tamarind liquid to make a smooth purée. Season with salt, put in a jar and keep in the refrigerator.

VIETNAMESE FISH SAUCE

2 red chilis
1 garlic clove, chopped
1 tsp sugar

1 lemon, peeled and sliced
2 tsp white wine vinegar
2 tsp water

Remove the stalks from the chilis, halve and remove the seeds. Chop roughly, then, using a pestle and mortar, crush with the garlic until a purée is obtained. Add the sugar. Gradually add the lemon slices to the chili purée and mash well. Lastly, add the vinegar and water and serve in a small bowl.

TAMARIND

This is the fruit of a tropical tree (Tamarindus indica), which is sold dried in packets. To use it, take a piece the size of a walnut and soak in about 100 ml/3¹/₂ fl oz of hot water for about 5 minutes. Knead with the fingers to dissolve the flesh in the water and remove the fibres and seeds.

CONVERSION TABLE

Weights and Measures

1 cup: 250 ml (¹/₄ litre)
¹/₂ cup: 125 ml (¹/₈ litre)
2 cups: 500 ml (¹/₂ litre)
3 cups: 750 ml (³/₄ litre)
4 cups: 1,000 ml (1 litre)
1 dessertspoon: 20 ml (4 teaspoons)
1 teaspoon: 5 ml

INDIA AND PAKISTAN

Hindustani cuisine is complex and very varied due to the numerous regions in this immense peninsula. The climate varies enormously from one region to another, as do the social, agricultural and ethnic conditions. In the north of India and in Pakistan the cooking is similar, the main difference being that the people of Pakistan are Muslims and therefore do not eat pork. Apart from this, both types of cuisine are characterized by strong spices, in particular the mixture known as 'curry'. Many Europeans presume that curry is always used in Hindustani dishes. However many different mixtures of spices and aromatic plants are blended by the Hindus to make their hot dishes which often come as a shock to the European palate.

Fatty lamb is the most commonly used meat. Food is usually cooked in butter or ghee, and meals are served with chapatis, made from wheat flour, as opposed to rice in other parts of the peninsula. Meat soups and broths are also common in this diet and are served with steamed vegetables, cut into small pieces and tossed with butter just before serving.

The strongest spices are used in Bangladesh, previously eastern Pakistan. Here, ghee is replaced by mustard oil, and fish and molluscs form the basis of cooking, rather than lamb.

Southern India has a very distinct cuisine, where coconut and rice are the basic foods. Rice replaces wheat in other regions; mustard grains and peppers are used frequently.

Religious restrictions influence Hindustani cooking quite significantly. Hindus do not eat beef, Buddhists do not eat any living creature or animal by-products, such as eggs, and many Indians are strict vegetarians.

Indian sweets and pastries are most original and very varied. In general, the main characteristic of Indian food is the variety of condiments that are served with the main dish.

SPICY DUCK WITH POTATOES AND CABBAGE

Serves 4

2 tbsp oil
1 large onion, peeled and chopped
4 cloves
4 cardamom pods
1 stick cinnamon
1 tsp ground turmeric
1 tsp grated ginger root
1/2 tsp ground black pepper
2 tsp ground coriander
1 x 2 kg/4 1/2 lb duck, jointed
2 fresh chilis, seeds removed
2 tsp salt
500 ml/18 fl oz hot water
2 tsp wine vinegar
4 potatoes, peeled and diced
1/2 cabbage, chopped
120 g/4 oz shelled peas

Heat the oil in a flameproof casserole and sauté the chopped onion. Add the cloves, cardamom and cinnamon, stirring until the onion is golden. Then add the turmeric, ginger, pepper and coriander. Sauté, stirring constantly for 2 minutes. Add the duck pieces and cook until golden. Add the whole, seeded chilis, salt, water and vinegar. Cover and simmer for 45 minutes until the duck is nearly cooked. Remove the grease from the sauce, add the diced potatoes and cook for another 10 minutes. Add the chopped cabbage and cook for another 10 minutes. Add the peas, season, cover and cook until the peas are tender. Serve hot.

PAKISTANI SALAD

Serves 6

1 lettuce
2 hard-boiled eggs, peeled and quartered
3 tomatoes, cut into 6 segments
sprig parsley, chopped
2 tsp chopped almonds

For the dressing:
3 tbsp oil
1 tbsp wine vinegar
1 tbsp salt
pinch pepper

Remove the outer leaves of the lettuce. Divide the remaining lettuce into leaves, wash and drain well. Arrange the lettuce leaves on a round serving dish to form a flower. Place the quartered hard-boiled eggs and the tomato segments in between the pieces of lettuce. Garnish with the chopped parsley and sprinkle with the chopped almonds. Serve cold with the sauce.

To make the dressing, combine all the ingredients together, mix thoroughly and place in a small jug.

Top: Mint Chutney
Bottom: Onion Sambal

RICE WITH LOBSTER, PAKISTANI-STYLE

Serves 6

2 x 500 g/1 lb 2 oz cooked lobsters
100 g/3 1/2 oz butter
2 onions, peeled and sliced
1 tbsp salt
1 tsp ground turmeric
1 tsp ground saffron
3 bay leaves
2 cloves
2 cinnamon sticks
500 g/1 lb 2 oz rice, washed and drained
6-8 mint leaves
300 ml/10 fl oz milk

Spice mix:
30 g/1 oz ginger root, crushed
30 g/1 oz green chili, finely chopped
1 tsp ground cinnamon
1/2 tsp powdered bay leaf
1/2 tsp cloves
2 tsp ground cumin
6 small tomatoes, halved

Cut each lobster into large chunks. Blend together the ingredients for the spice mix.

Melt the butter in an ovenproof casserole and sauté half the sliced onions over a low heat. Add the spice mix and 2 teaspoons of the salt, stir, then add half the turmeric and saffron. Sauté over a low heat and add the lobsters just before the mixture starts to go golden. Cover and cook for 10 minutes, stirring occasionally.

Meanwhile, fill a saucepan with cold water. Add the bay leaves, cloves, cinnamon sticks and remaining salt. Bring to the boil over a high heat. Add the rice and stir with a wooden spatula. Cover and leave to cook. When the rice is half-cooked, drain, remove the flavourings, and reserve.

Preheat the oven to 170° C/325° F, gas mark 3. Boil 100 ml/3 1/2 fl oz water in a small pan with the remaining turmeric and saffron. Add some of the par-boiled rice to the lobster, then add half the turmeric and saffron water, the mint leaves, the second portion of rice and the remaining sliced onion. Pour the rest of the turmeric and saffron water over the top. Slowly pour the milk round the edges of the dish. Cover and cook in the oven for 1 hour or until the rice has absorbed all the liquid.

SPICY RICE WITH PRAWNS

Serves 4

500 g/1 lb 2 oz raw prawns
250 g/9 oz long-grain rice
★45 g/1 1/2 oz ghee
1 tbsp oil
1 onion, peeled and chopped
3 garlic cloves, chopped
1/2 tsp grated ginger root
4 cardamom pods
1 stick cinnamon
★1 tsp garam masala
1/2 tsp cayenne
2 red chilis, chopped
1 1/2 tsp salt
750 ml/1 1/4 pints hot water
1/2 cucumber, sliced
sprig of fresh coriander leaves, chopped

Peel the prawns and remove the black vein in the centre of the back. Wash the rice and drain well.

Heat the ghee and oil in a large pan with a lid. Briefly sauté the prawns until they begin to colour, then set aside.

Add the chopped onion, garlic and ginger to the pan and sauté for several minutes, stirring frequently. Add the rice, cardamom and cinnamon and sauté until blended with the ghee. Add the garam masala, cayenne, chilis, salt, prawns and hot water. Bring to the boil, cover and cook for 20 minutes. Serve hot, garnished with cucumber slices and sprinkled with chopped coriander leaves.

KASHMIR LAMB

Serves 6

1 kg/2 1/4 lb lean lamb
225 ml/8 fl oz yoghurt
★30 g/1 oz ghee
2 tsp salt
1 tsp ground ginger
500 ml/18 fl oz hot water
1 tsp cayenne
2 tsp grated ginger root
★2 tsp garam masala
1 tbsp chopped coriander leaves

Cut any fat off the meat and cut into cubes.

Mix together the yoghurt, ghee, salt and ginger and place in a flameproof casserole. Add the lamb, cover and cook for about 1 hour, stirring occasionally. After a short while, the juices from the meat will have evaporated and the spices will begin to stick to the dish. To avoid this, add 100 ml/3 1/2 fl oz of the hot water, together with the cayenne and ginger. Mix well

with a wooden spoon, scraping the bottom of the pan.

Continue cooking until the liquid evaporates again and the mixture begins to stick, then add the same amount of water. Repeat this operation until the meat is very tender and the liquid has evaporated. Sprinkle the garam masala and chopped coriander leaves over the meat. Cover again and cook over a low heat for 10-15 minutes. Serve hot with rice or chapatis.

Top: Rice with Lobster, Pakistani-style
Bottom: Spicy Rice with Prawns

BENGALI RICE

Serves 4

500 ml/17 fl oz milk
225 ml/8 fl oz water
1 coconut, grated
1 tsp salt
1 tsp sugar
3 tbsp olive oil
1 onion, peeled and chopped
4 tsp curry powder
4 tsp apple purée
100 g/3½ oz rice

Mix the milk with the water to prevent the milk sticking or boiling over. Heat the liquid in a pan. Add the grated coconut, salt and sugar and bring to the boil. Remove from the heat and leave the coconut to absorb the liquid for 15 minutes. Strain through a sieve and leave the coconut to drain on some kitchen roll, reserving the liquid that is drained off.

Heat half the oil in a pan and sauté the chopped onion. Add the curry powder, stir, then add the apple purée and stir well.

Wash the rice several times, drain, then add to the pan and heat, stirring well. Add the reserved coconut liquid and leave to cook for 15 minutes. The rice should absorb the liquid.

Sauté the drained coconut in the remaining oil before adding the rest of the mixture.

This dish is usually served with roast chicken pieces and some mustard and mango chutney.

EGG CURRY WITH LENTILS

Serves 4

4 onions, peeled and chopped
2 garlic cloves, crushed
4 tsp curry powder
1 apple, peeled and chopped
60 g/2 oz chicken fat or butter
160 g/6 oz split red lentils
2 tsp salt
4 hard-boiled eggs, peeled and sliced
2 tsp chopped, mixed herbs

Sauté the chopped onions, garlic, curry powder and apple in half the chicken fat or butter until soft.

Meanwhile, wash the lentils and cook in twice their volume of boiling, salted water. The water should evaporate and be partially absorbed by the lentils. After

about 20 minutes, add the remaining chicken fat or butter, cut into pieces, then the sliced hard-boiled eggs. Add the chopped herbs and continue to cook, stirring until the mixture comes to the boil.

Serve with baked potatoes or buttered bread.

FISH CURRY WITH TOMATO

Serves 4

500 g/1 lb 2 oz fish fillets (e.g. cod, whiting), skinned
★4 tsp ghee or vegetable oil
1 medium onion, peeled and chopped
2 garlic cloves, chopped
4 tsp chopped mint leaves
1 tsp ground cumin
1 tsp ground turmeric

1 tsp cayenne
1 large ripe tomato, skinned, seeded and chopped
1 tsp salt
★1¹/₂ tsp garam masala
lemon juice to taste

Cut the fish into chunks. Heat the ghee or oil in a frying-pan with a lid and lightly sauté the chopped onion, garlic and mint leaves, stirring constantly until the onion is golden. Add the cumin, turmeric and cayenne and stir for 3 minutes until the spices are cooked. Add the chopped tomato, salt and garam masala. Sauté, stirring, until the tomato is has turned into purée. Season and add lemon juice to taste. Stir the chunks of fish into the sauce, cover and simmer for 10 minutes until the fish is cooked. Serve with rice.

Left: Bengali Rice
Below: Fish Curry with Tomato

SEASONED WHITE RICE

Serves 4

225 g/8 oz long-grain rice
*2 tsp ghee
750 ml/1¼ pints hot water
1 tsp salt

Wash the rice and leave to drain in a colander for 30 minutes. Heat the ghee in a saucepan, add the rice and sauté for 2 minutes, stirring constantly. Add the hot water and salt, mix well and bring to the boil. Cover and cook over a low heat for 20 minutes, without removing the lid or stirring. Then remove the lid and allow the steam to escape for 1-2 minutes. Stir gently with a fork to separate the grains. Place the rice in a dish and fork through.

When this rice is used instead of bread, as is often the case in most of India and Pakistan, the amount stated above will only be enough to serve two.

LAMB CURRY

Serves 6

*4 tsp ghee or oil
2 large onions, peeled and chopped
4 garlic cloves, crushed
2 tsp chopped ginger root
*4 tsp curry powder
2 tsp salt
4 tsp wine vinegar
1.5 kg/3¼ lb boned leg of lamb, cubed
3 large tomatoes, skinned, seeded and chopped
2 whole chilis
2 tbsp chopped mint leaves
*2 tsp garam masala

Heat the ghee or oil in a flameproof casserole dish and sauté the chopped onion, garlic and ginger. Add the curry powder, salt and vinegar and mix well. Add the cubed lamb and sauté, stirring constantly until the meat is covered with the spices. Then add the chopped tomatoes, whole chilis and all but 2 teaspoons of the chopped mint leaves. Cover and cook for about 1½ hours over a low heat, stirring occasionally. The juice from the tomatoes should ensure that the meat does not stick, but if it does, add a little hot water while it is cooking.

Five minutes before the end of cooking time, add the garam masala and the remaining chopped mint leaves.

GULAB JAMAN

Serves 4
150 g/5 oz powdered milk
2 tsp flour
½ tsp baking powder
10 tsp water
225 g/8 oz butter
100 g/3½ oz sugar
500 ml/18 fl oz water for cooking

Combine the powdered milk, flour, baking powder and 10 tsp water in a bowl to make a soft dough. Divide the dough into balls, roughly the size of plums. Heat the butter in a frying-pan and gently fry the dough balls for 4–5 minutes, turning constantly, until cooked through. Meanwhile, dissolve the sugar in 500 ml/18 fl oz water then simmer to obtain a thick syrup. Drain the balls, place in the syrup and leave for several hours. Serve cold or slightly warm.

This is a delicious sweet dish, eaten frequently in India.

CUCUMBER IN YOGHURT

Serves 4

2 cucumbers, peeled and chopped
2 tsp white wine vinegar
4 tsp sugar
1 tsp salt
4 tomatoes, skinned, seeded and chopped
2 onions, peeled and chopped
1 green pepper, seeded and finely chopped
½ tsp mustard powder
300 ml/10 fl oz natural yoghurt
1 tbsp chopped parsley

Place the chopped cucumber in a colander, sprinkle with the vinegar, sugar and salt and leave to stand for 10 minutes to extract the moisture. Place most of the chopped tomatoes in a serving bowl, reserving a few pieces for garnish. Stir in the chopped onions, pepper, mustard powder and yoghurt. Add the cucumbers and top with the reserved tomatoes and chopped parsley.

STUFFED PEPPERS

Serves 6

500 g/1 lb 2 oz potatoes, peeled and chopped
2 tbsp oil
250 g/9 oz minced chicken meat
2 medium onions, peeled and chopped
2 tsp salt
½ tsp ground cardamom
½ tsp ground coriander
½ tsp ground cinnamon
½ tsp ground cloves
12 small red peppers, halved, seeded and skinned

Cook the chopped potatoes in boiling water. Drain, return to the pan and cook over a high heat, mashing to obtain a purée.

Preheat the oven to 180° C/350° F, gas mark 4. In a small frying-pan, heat one third of the oil and fry the chicken, stirring, for 5 minutes. Stir in the potatoes, onions, salt and spices to make the stuffing. Stuff the peppers with the mixture and place in an ovenproof dish. Pour on the remaining oil and bake in the oven for 20 minutes. Serve garnished with shredded red cabbage (optional).

Top: Cucumbers in Yoghurt
Bottom: Stuffed Peppers

TANDOURI POUSSIN

Serves 4

2 x 700 g/1½ lb poussin
225 ml/8 fl oz strained yoghurt
½ tsp ground saffron
1 tsp grated ginger root
3 garlic cloves, crushed
1½ tsp paprika
1½ tsp ground cumin
1½ tsp ground cardamom
1 tsp ground cinnamon
1 tsp cayenne
2 tsp salt
2 tbsp melted butter

Make a few cuts in the breasts, wings and thighs of the whole poussins and rub salt into them.

Mix the remaining ingredients together except for the butter. The saffron will give colour to the dish. Paint the poussins with this mixture, using a brush, and leave to stand overnight in the refrigerator. The following day, preheat the oven to 200° C/400° F, gas mark 6, place the poussins on a rack over a roasting tin and cook in the oven for 40 minutes until the

**Top: Poori
Bottom: Hindustani Mulligatawny Soup**

meat is tender. Pour over the melted butter and roast for a further 5 minutes. Cut the poussins in half and serve immediately.

POORI

Serves 4

60 g/2 oz plain flour
60 g/2 oz wholewheat flour
4 tsp vegetable oil
100 ml/3½ fl oz water
oil for deep-frying, as required

Place the flours in a mixing bowl. Add the oil and enough water to make a dough. Knead well, cover with a damp teatowel and leave to stand for 3 hours.

Roll the dough into a long sausage shape and cut into slices. Flatten the slices with your hands to about 2.5 cm/1 inch thickness.

Heat the oil in a deep frying-pan. Fry the slices of dough in the hot oil until they are puffed up and crunchy.

HINDUSTANI MULLIGATAWNY SOUP

Serves 4

1 chicken
1 onion, peeled and quartered
1 bouquet garni
1 bay leaf
1 tsp salt
45 g/1½ oz butter
75 g/2½ oz smoked bacon, derinded and sliced
4 tomatoes, skinned, seeded and chopped
45 g/1½ oz flour
2 tsp curry powder
pinch cayenne
100 ml/3½ fl oz single cream

Place the chicken in a large pan with just enough water to cover. Add the onion quarters, bouquet garni, bay leaf and salt. Bring to the boil, then cover and simmer gently for about 2 hours, depending on the size of the bird. Remove the chicken from the liquid, discard the skin and cut the meat into strips. Strain the cooking liquid and reserve.

Heat the butter in a large saucepan and fry the bacon and tomatoes. Sprinkle in the flour, stirring well, and gradually add the strained cooking liquid. Simmer for 15 minutes and season with the curry powder and cayenne. Add the chicken meat and heat through. Stir in the cream and serve hot with croûtons, if desired.

**Top: Poori
Bottom: Hindustani Mulligatawny Soup**

RICE BLANCMANGE

Serves 4

2 tbsp ground rice
750 ml/1¼ pints milk
2 tbsp sugar
½ tsp ground cardamom
2 tsp rosewater
4 tsp peeled pistachios, chopped

Mix the ground rice with a little cold milk to make a smooth paste.

Heat the remaining milk with the sugar, stirring with a wooden spoon. Add the ground rice paste and cook over a low heat, stirring constantly, until the mixture thickens. Simmer for 3 minutes, sprinkle with the cardamom, add the rosewater and half the chopped pistachios. Mix well and serve in small bowls topped with the remaining pistachios. May be served hot or chilled.

HINDU BISCUITS

Serves 4

200 g/7 oz flour
200 g/7 oz cornflour
10 g/⅓ oz fresh yeast
2 tsp tepid water
★100 ml/3½ fl oz coconut milk
pinch of salt
pinch of ground cinnamon
pinch of grated nutmeg
1 tsp vanilla essence
1 egg yolk, beaten

Preheat the oven to 220° C/425° F, gas mark 7. Place the flours in a mixing bowl, mix well and make a well in the centre. Cream the yeast with the water and pour into the well. Add the coconut milk, salt, cinnamon, nutmeg and vanilla essence. Mix well together and knead to form a dough. Roll out the dough to ½ cm/¼ inch thickness. Cut into circles using a small glass and place the circles on a greased baking tray. Brush with beaten egg yolk and bake in the oven for 20 minutes.

CHICKEN CURRY WITH YOGHURT

Serves 4

★1½ tsp ghee or oil
1 medium onion, peeled and chopped
3 garlic cloves, crushed
30 g/1 oz mint leaves
1 tsp grated ginger root
1 tsp ground turmeric
★1½ tsp garam masala

Top: Rice Blancmange
Bottom: Hindu Biscuits

pinch of salt
1½ tsp cayenne (optional)
100 ml/3½ fl oz yoghurt
2 ripe tomatoes, skinned, seeded and chopped
1 x 1 kg/2¼ lb chicken, jointed

Heat the ghee or oil in a flameproof casserole and sauté the chopped onion, garlic and mint leaves for 5 minutes, stirring constantly. Add the ginger, turmeric, garam masala, salt and cayenne (if using) and sauté lightly for 1 minute. Add the yoghurt and chopped tomatoes and cook, stirring constantly, until the mixture becomes a thick purée. Then add the chicken pieces, mixing well to cover them with the sauce. Cover and simmer

gently for about 40 minutes until the chicken is tender.

If the sauce is too thin, remove the lid and cook briskly for a few minutes, stirring to avoid sticking.

To serve, garnish with chopped mint leaves and serve with rice or chapatis.

LAMB KEBABS

Serves 6

500 g/1 lb 2 oz boned shoulder of lamb
2 tsp desiccated coconut
1 large onion, peeled and chopped
2 garlic cloves, crushed
1 tsp grated ginger root
1/4 tsp grated nutmeg
1/4 tsp ground cinnamon
1/4 tsp ground cloves
1/4 tsp ground cardamom
1/2 tsp ground black pepper
1 tsp poppy seeds
100 ml/3 1/2 fl oz yoghurt

Cut the lamb into 4 cm/1 1/2 inch cubes and place in a non-enamel dish. Toast the coconut in a dry frying-pan over a moderate heat, stirring constantly, until golden. Leave to cool. Liquidize the chopped onion, garlic and ginger to make a paste. Add the spices, coconut, poppy seeds and yoghurt and blend again. Pour this mixture over the meat, turning the pieces over and covering them completely. Cover and chill overnight, or for at least 2 hours at room temperature.

Divide the pieces of meat between 6 metal or bamboo skewers. Cook under a hot grill or over charcoal, turning occasionally, for about 10 minutes. Serve with chapatis or rice, onion sambal and mint chutney.

SABJI SALAD

Serves 6

For the salad:
2 large onions, peeled and finely chopped
2 large tomatoes, skinned, seeded and sliced
6 sprigs parsley, finely chopped
2 red peppers, seeded and sliced

For the dressing:
1/2 small onion, peeled and finely chopped
1 small tomato, skinned, seeded and finely chopped
3 tbsp wine vinegar
1 tsp salt
1/2 tsp sugar

To make the dressing, place all the

dressing ingredients in a small mixing bowl. Stir well and refrigerate until ready to use.

To make the salad, arrange all the salad ingredients in a serving dish. Chill for 1 hour then pour on the dressing just before serving.

CHAPATIS

Makes 20

700 g/1 1/2 lb wholemeal flour
1 heaped tsp salt
*2 tsp ghee or oil (optional)
225 ml/8 fl oz tepid water

Reserve 90 g/3 oz of the flour for rolling out the chapati dough and place the remainder in a large mixing bowl. Add the salt and mix, then add the ghee or oil, if using. Add all the water at once and mix to obtain a firm dough. Knead for 10 minutes (the longer it is kneaded, the lighter the chapatis will be). Shape the dough into a ball, cover with clingfilm, and leave to stand for at least 1 hour. If the dough is left to stand overnight, the texture of the chapatis will be even lighter and crisper.

Divide the dough into balls the size of a walnut and roll out on a floured surface to the size of a pancake. Cook the chapatis in a dry frying-pan one by one, for 1 minute on each side, pressing lightly round the edges with a rolled cloth or a spatula. This encourages air pockets to form and inflate the chapati.

When all the chapatis are ready, wrap in a cloth to keep them hot. Serve with butter to accompany dry curry and vegetable dishes.

PORK VINDALOO

Serves 6

6 large, dried red chilis
225 ml/8 fl oz wine vinegar
2 tsp chopped ginger root
6 garlic cloves, chopped
2 tsp ground cumin
1/2 tsp ground black pepper
1/2 tsp ground cinnamon
1/2 tsp ground cardamom
1/4 tsp ground cloves
1/4 tsp grated nutmeg
3 tsp salt
1 kg/2 1/4 lb lean pork, cubed
2 tbsp oil
2 onions, peeled and chopped
2 tsp brown sugar (optional)

Soak the chilis in the vinegar for at least 10 minutes, or longer if a stronger flavour is required. Remove the chilis from the vinegar and chop finely. Combine with the ginger, garlic, spices and salt. Place the meat in a non-metallic dish, pour over the spice mixture and leave to marinate for 2 hours.

Heat the oil and sauté the chopped onions over medium heat until golden. Drain the meat, add to the pan and sauté until golden. Stir in the marinade, cover and simmer over a low heat for about 1 hour until the meat is tender. Add the brown sugar, if desired, and serve with white rice.

Top: Sabji Salad
Bottom: Grilled Lamb Madura-style
(recipe on page 37)

PRAWNS IN COCONUT MILK

Serves 4

700 g/1½ lb raw prawns, peeled
*2 tsp ghee or oil
2 medium onions, peeled and chopped
2 garlic cloves, crushed
1 tsp grated ginger root
2 red or green chilis, seeded and chopped
*8 curry leaves, chopped
1 tsp ground turmeric
*500 ml/18 fl oz coconut milk
1 tsp salt
lemon juice to taste

Leave the prawns whole or chop roughly, if preferred. Heat the ghee or oil and sauté the chopped onion, garlic and ginger, until soft but not coloured. Add the chopped chilis, curry leaves and turmeric. Sauté for one minute, then add the coconut milk and salt. Bring to the boil, stirring constantly, then simmer for 10 minutes uncovered. Add the prawns and cook for another 10–15 minutes.

Remove the pan from the heat and add lemon juice to taste. Serve immediately, garnished with extra chopped curry leaves, if desired.

CALCUTTA-STYLE STEW

Serves 4

60 g/2 oz butter
250 g/9 oz stewing beef, sliced
3 onions, peeled and finely sliced
¼ celeriac, peeled and chopped
2 carrots, peeled and sliced
1 small cauliflower, divided into florets
90 g/3 oz shelled peas
1 celery stalk, chopped
250 g/9 oz green beans, halved
500 ml/18 fl oz stock
4 tsp grated coconut
½ tsp cayenne
1½ tsp salt
½ tsp curry powder

Melt the butter in a flameproof casserole dish and brown the sliced beef over a high heat. Add the vegetables and cook for 2 minutes, stirring. Pour in the stock, cover and cook for about 1 hour until the beef and vegetables are tender. Shortly before the end of cooking time, add the grated coconut, cayenne, salt and curry powder. The sauce should not be too thick.

When serving, the dish may be topped with some toasted French bread rubbed with garlic. An alternative way of preparing the dish is to shape the meat into meatballs and cook them separately before adding to the other ingredients.

AUBERGINES WITH YOGHURT

Serves 6

2 medium aubergines
★2 tbsp ghee or oil
2 onions, peeled and chopped
3 garlic cloves, chopped
2 tsp grated ginger root
2 tsp ground coriander
1 tsp ground cumin
$1/2$ tsp ground turmeric
$1/2$ tsp cayenne
$11/2$ tsp salt
★$1/2$ tsp garam masala (optional)
2 tsp sugar (optional)
225 ml/8 fl oz yoghurt

Grill the aubergines under medium heat for about 6 minutes, then increase the heat and cook until the skin is blackened and the flesh soft – about 20-25 minutes.

Allow to cool, remove the skins and finely chop the flesh.

Heat the ghee or oil in a large saucepan and sauté the chopped onions, garlic and ginger. Add the coriander, cumin, turmeric and cayenne and sauté for 1 minute, stirring continuously. Add the chopped aubergine and salt and fry for 3-4 minutes, stirring constantly. Stir in the garam masala, if using, cover and cook for 5 minutes. Taste and adjust the seasoning and add the sugar, if using. Beat the yoghurt and add to the aubergine mixture just before serving. This dish is usually served with rice or as an accompaniment to other dishes.

**Opposite: Calcutta-style Stew
Above: Prawns in Coconut Milk**

SRI LANKA

For a long time, the beautiful island of Ceylon was considered as part of India, but since it won independence several years ago, it has been known as Sri Lanka.

The basic food of Sri Lanka is rice, almost always served with curry which is abundant in soups, fish, meat and vegetable dishes. The Singhalese have achieved perfection when it comes to making this mix of spices. In Sri Lanka there are white, red and black curries, the latter being the most delicious.

RED PORK CURRY

Serves 8

8 dried red chilis, seeded
300 ml/10 fl oz hot water
2 tsp tamarind pulp
1/2 tsp ground turmeric
1 medium onion, peeled and chopped
5 garlic cloves, chopped
1 tbsp chopped ginger root
1 kg/2 1/4 lb pork tenderloin, cubed
1 cinnamon stick
2 tsp salt
grated rind of 2 lemons
8 curry leaves, chopped
1/4 tsp fenugreek seeds
*500 ml/18 fl oz coconut milk
*2 tsp ghee or oil
1 small onion, peeled and chopped
60 g/2 oz canned sweetcorn
4 tsp lemon juice

Soak the chilis in half the hot water for 10 minutes. Soak the tamarind pulp in the remaining hot water.

Place the chilis and their liquid in a liquidizer with the turmeric, chopped medium onion, garlic and ginger and blend to a purée.

Place the meat in a flameproof casserole and pour over the purée. Add the cinnamon, and strained tamarind liquid. Season with salt then add half the grated lemon rind, and half the curry leaves and fenugreek seeds. Bring to the boil, cover and cook over a low heat for about 1 hour until the meat is tender. Add the coconut milk and cook for 10 minutes uncovered.

Sauté the small chopped onion in hot ghee or oil with the remaining lemon rind, curry leaves, fenugreek and sweetcorn. Add to the pork with the lemon juice, stir well and simmer for 5 minutes. Serve with rice and other side dishes.

FISH CURRY WITH TAMARIND

Serves 2

1 tbsp tamarind pulp
100 ml/3 1/2 fl oz hot water
1 1/2 tsp curry powder
1 tsp salt
1/4 tsp ground turmeric
1 tsp cayenne
500 g/1 lb 2 oz cod or haddock fillets, cubed
2 tbsp oil
6 curry leaves, chopped
1/4 tsp fenugreek seeds
1 onion, peeled and finely chopped
2 garlic cloves, finely chopped

Place the tamarind pulp in a small bowl, pour over the hot water and leave to cool. Blend to a purée in a liquidizer, then mix with the curry powder, salt, turmeric and cayenne. Marinate the fish in this mixture for 20 minutes.

Heat the oil in a frying-pan and sauté the curry leaves and fenugreek for 20 minutes. Add the onion and garlic and continue to sauté over a moderate heat, stirring occasionally. When the onion is golden, add the fish and the marinade, cover and leave to cook over a low heat for 10 minutes. Uncover and cook for a further 10 minutes.

Serve hot with rice and vegetable curry.

SINGHALESE CURRY POWDER

170 g/6 oz coriander seeds
90 g/3 oz fennel seeds
1 tsp fenugreek seeds
1 x 5 cm/2 inch stick of cinnamon
1 tsp whole cloves
1 tsp cardamom seeds
4 tsp dried curry leaves
2 tsp cayenne
4 tsp ground rice

Toast the coriander, fennel and fenugreek seeds separately in a dry frying-pan, stirring constantly, until the spices take on a dark brown colour, but making sure they do not burn.

Grind the toasted seeds to a fine powder with the cinnamon stick, cloves, cardamom and curry leaves. Add the cayenne and ground rice. This stores well in an airtight jar.

Top: Sinhalese Curry Powder
Bottom: Red Pork Curry

VEGETABLE CURRY

Serves 6

*750 ml/1¼ pints coconut milk
1 onion, peeled and finely chopped
2 green chilis, halved and seeded
2 garlic cloves, finely chopped
½ tsp ground turmeric
½ tsp grated ginger root
1 x 5 cm/2 inch cinnamon stick
grated rind of 2 lemons
8 curry leaves, chopped
700 g/1½ lb mixed vegetables, chopped
1 tsp salt
*225 ml/8 fl oz coconut cream

Place all the ingredients, except the mixed vegetables, salt and coconut cream in a large saucepan. Bring to the boil and simmer for 10 minutes. Add the chopped mixed vegetables and salt, bring to the boil again and simmer over a low heat for about 20 minutes until the vegetables are tender. Add the coconut cream and cook for another 5 minutes.

This curry is usually served as a side dish.

SINGHALESE EGG ROLLS

Serves 8

6 eggs
500 g/1 lb 2 oz potatoes, peeled and diced
pinch of nutmeg
5 green chilis, seeded and finely chopped
2 tsp chopped ginger root
1 tsp salt
½ tsp ground black pepper
120 g/4 oz breadcrumbs
oil for frying

Hard-boil 4 of the eggs, peel and cut into quarters. Separate the whites from the yolks of the remaining 2 eggs and dilute the whites with 2 teaspoons of water.

Boil the potatoes, drain well and dry in the pan over the heat. Mash the potatoes to a purée then add the nutmeg, chilis, ginger, salt, pepper and egg yolks. Mix well together.

Divide the mixture into 16 equal amounts and form into short, fat rolls. Push an egg quarter into the middle of each and re-form. Brush each roll with the diluted egg whites and coat with breadcrumbs. Fry in very hot oil until golden and serve hot.

YELLOW SINGHALESE RICE

Serves 6

500 g/1 lb 2 oz long-grain rice
*3 tbsp ghee
2 onions, peeled and chopped
6 cloves
20 black peppercorns
12 cardamom pods, crushed
1½ tsp ground turmeric
12 curry leaves
sprig of lemon balm, chopped
3½ tsp salt
*2 litres/3½ pints coconut milk

Wash the rice and drain well. Heat the ghee in a large saucepan and sauté the chopped onions. Add the cloves, peppercorns, cardamom pods, turmeric, curry leaves, balm and salt.

Add the rice and sauté for 2-3 minutes, stirring until the grains are covered with ghee and turmeric. Then add the coconut milk and bring to the boil. Reduce the heat, cover and leave to cook for 20-25 minutes without removing the lid.

When the rice is cooked, the spices should all rise to the surface. Remove the spices and curry leaves and stir the rice carefully, using a fork. Serve hot with a main dish, particularly a curry and its accompaniments.

Top: Vegetable Curry
Bottom: Singhalese Egg Rolls

SESAME AND PALM-SUGAR BALLS

Makes

350 g/12 oz sesame seeds
500 g/1 lb 2 oz palm sugar, grated
pinch of salt
extra sesame seeds for coating

If palm sugar is unobtainable, use brown sugar or maple syrup.

Pound the sesame seeds in small amounts using a pestle and mortar. The end result should be an oily paste. Add the sugar or syrup and salt and mix well with your hands until the sugar melts slightly. Roll the mixture into balls the size of a large marble. Coat the balls in sesame seeds and place in individual paper sweet cases.

Serve at the end of a main meal such as curry, or eat as a snack.

SINGHALESE LOVE-CAKE

120 g/4 oz butter
250 g/9 oz semolina
10 egg yolks
500 g/1 lb 2 oz castor sugar
170 g/6 oz unsalted cashew nuts, finely chopped
1/4 tsp grated lemon rind
4 tsp rosewater
1 tbsp honey
1/4 tsp grated nutmeg
1/4 tsp ground cinnamon

Preheat the oven to 170° C/325° F, gas mark 3. Place the butter in a mixing bowl, soften with a wooden spoon, then add the semolina. Beat the egg yolks with the sugar until creamy. Add to the semolina mixture and blend well. Stir in the chopped cashew nuts, grated lemon rind, rosewater, honey, nutmeg and cinnamon. Mix together well and turn into a shallow round cake tin lined with greaseproof paper, and greased with butter. There should be enough room left for the mixture to rise. Bake in the oven for 1 hour until the cake is golden and cooked through. Turn on to a wire cake rack to cool. Decorate with piped cream and orange slices.

Top: Sesame and Palm Sugar Balls
Bottom: Singhalese Love-Cake

INDONESIA

Made up of over one thousand islands, the Indonesian archipelago stretches between continental Asia and Australia. It is an exotic land of green equatorial jungle and humid heat. Throughout Indonesia's history, its islands have represented a meeting place for many different peoples and cultures, such as the Chinese, the Hindus, the Malaysians, the Portuguese, the Dutch and the English. As a result of this mixture of customs, Indonesian cuisine is one of the finest in the world, and yet it is unknown in most western countries. Many of the strongly flavoured dishes taste strange to the European palate. In fact Indonesian cuisine is a masterful blend of savoury, sour, bitter and sweet flavours, usually combined in a subtle way so that no single flavour predominates.

The basic component of Indonesian cooking is rice, usually steamed, which enables it to take on the flavour of spices and gives it a pearly appearance. With rice, Indonesians serve a wide variety of curries made with fish, meat and poultry. They also serve vegetable dishes - fried, boiled or in salads. The word 'sambal' describes anything that is fried with a lot of chili pepper. There are sambals made with prawns, chicken or ox, etc.

All the dishes that make up a meal are served at the same time, except for sweets and fruits. All the dishes are arranged around the rice, which is the basis of the meal. Food is eaten with the hands, an art which the Indonesians have perfected, using only the tips of the fingers of the right hand. Hands are washed afterwards in a finger bowl with some slices of lemon.

PEANUT CRUNCHES

90 g/3 oz rice flour
4 tsp ground rice
1/2 tsp ground cumin
1 tsp ground coriander
1/4 tsp ground turmeric
1 tsp salt
★225 ml/8 fl oz coconut milk
1 garlic clove, crushed
1 small onion, peeled and finely chopped
120 g/4 oz roasted unsalted peanuts, roughly chopped
oil for frying, as needed

Mix all the dry ingredients together in a bowl. Add the coconut milk and beat until a smooth paste is obtained. Add the garlic, onion and peanuts. Heat oil 1 cm/1/2 inch deep in a frying-pan. When the oil is hot, put 1 tablespoon of the mixture into it and fry on both sides. Continue cooking one spoonful at a time until all the mixture is used up. Drain on kitchen towel on a cooling rack, so that the discs will remain crunchy. Allow to cool then store in an airtight container. Serve with rice dishes and curries or as a starter.

PRAWN SAMBAL WITH COCONUT MILK

Serves 4

500 g/1 lb 2 oz raw prawns
4 tsp peanut oil
6 curry leaves
1 onion, peeled and finely chopped
2 fresh red chilis, seeded and chopped
3 garlic cloves, chopped
★1/2 tsp sambal-ulek
1/2 tsp ground galingale
100 ml/31/2 fl oz prawn stock
★30 g/1 oz coconut cream
1 tsp salt
1/2 tsp brown sugar

Peel the prawns and use the heads and the peelings to make the prawn stock. Heat the oil in a frying-pan and sauté the curry leaves, onion, chilis and garlic until golden. Add the sambal-ulek and the galingale and sauté for a few seconds. Add the prawns and sauté until they take on colour.

Add the prawn stock, coconut cream, salt and sugar, and simmer, uncovered until the liquid thickens and the oil separates from the mixture. Serve with rice and curry.

TAMARIND PORK, BALINESE-STYLE

Serves 4

500 g/1 lb 2 oz loin of pork
1 onion, peeled and chopped
2 garlic cloves, chopped
2 tsp grated ginger root
2 fresh red chilis, seeded
4 tsp thick soya sauce
1 tbsp oil
3 tbsp liquid tamarind
1/2 tsp salt
2 tsp brown sugar

Cut the pork into strips 5 cm/2 inches wide. Mix together the onion, garlic, ginger, chilis and soya sauce. Heat the oil in a frying-pan and sauté the pork pieces over a low heat. Drain off the excess oil and add the onion and chili mixture to the pork. Cook for 4–5 minutes over a moderate heat. Add the liquid tamarind, salt and about 60 ml/2 fl oz hot water. Cover the pan and simmer for 25–30 minutes. Add the sugar and continue cooking uncovered, until the sauce becomes dark brown and reduced. Serve hot.

Top: Prawn Sambal with Coconut Milk
Bottom: Tamarind Pork, Balinese-style

SQUID CURRY

Serves 6

500 g/1 lb 2 oz squid
1 onion, peeled and chopped
2 garlic cloves, crushed
1 tsp grated ginger root
1 tsp salt
1 tsp cayenne
★1/2 tsp dried shrimp paste
★300 ml/10 fl oz coconut milk
★1 candlenut or Brazil nut, grated
1 tsp grated lemon rind
1 tsp brown sugar
3 tbsp lemon juice

Remove the head, tentacles and ink-sac from the squid. Pull off and discard the mottled skin. Slice the remaining flesh into cubes and roughly chop the tentacles.

Place the rest of the ingredients, except the sugar and lemon juice, in a saucepan. Bring to the boil, and cook, stirring, until it reduces a little. Add the squid and cook for a further 5-6 minutes. Stir in the sugar and lemon juice, taste and adjust the seasoning. Serve hot with rice and vegetables. As a variation, sliced red pepper may be added to the onion mixture.

FRIED JAVANESE CHICKEN

Serves 4

1 x 1.5 kg/3¼ lb chicken
1 onion, peeled and chopped
3 garlic cloves
3 red chilis, seeded and chopped
2 tsp grated ginger root
grated rind of 2 lemons
★500 ml/18 fl oz coconut milk
1/2 tsp ground turmeric
1 tsp ground black pepper
2 tsp ground coriander
1 1/2 tsp salt
4 curry leaves
2 lemon tree leaves (optional)

Cut the chicken in half and press down to flatten. Place the onion, garlic, chilis, ginger and lemon rind in a liquidizer and blend to a purée. Add 1-2 tablespoons of the coconut milk and blend again. Add the turmeric, pepper, coriander, salt and another tablespoon of coconut milk. Blend again for a few seconds. Coat the chicken with half the mixture and leave to

Left: Squid Curry
Right: Fried Javanese Chicken

marinate in the coating for at least
30 minutes.

Place the remaining paste in a frying-pan
with the curry and lemon tree leaves, if
using. Swill the blender out with a little of
the coconut milk and pour this and the
remaining coconut milk into the frying-
pan. Bring to the boil, stirring constantly,
then add the chicken and simmer for 10
minutes, basting from time to time. Turn
the chicken over and simmer for 30
minutes until tender. Remove the chicken
and cook under a preheated medium grill
or on a barbecue for 10-15 minutes,
turning once. Meanwhile, simmer the
sauce to reduce slightly.

When the chicken is well grilled on
both sides, place on a serving dish and
cover with the sauce. Serve the remaining
sauce in a jug separately.

FISH, BALINESE-STYLE

Serves 6

700 g/1½ lb firm white fish fillets (e.g. cod or
haddock)
peanut oil, for frying
2 onions, peeled and chopped
2 garlic cloves, chopped
1½ tsp grated ginger root
★1 tsp sambal-ulek
1 tsp grated lemon rind
4 tsp lemon juice
1 tsp ground galingale
4 tsp brown sugar
4 tsp thick soya sauce
½ tsp salt

Cut the fish into medium-sized pieces.
Heat 2 tablespoons of oil in a small pan
and sauté the onions until completely
softened. Add the garlic and ginger and
sauté over a medium heat, stirring
constantly. When the onions are golden,
add the sambal-ulek, grated lemon rind,
lemon juice, galingale, sugar, soya sauce
and salt. Simmer for 2-3 minutes, then
set aside.

In a deep fat fryer, heat the peanut oil to
190° C/375° F or until a cube of stale
bread turns golden in 30 seconds. Fry the
pieces of fish until golden. Drain the fish,
arrange on a serving dish and cover with
the sauce.

VEGETABLES WITH COCONUT SAUCE

Serves 6

700 g/1½ lb mixed vegetables
1 onion, peeled and chopped
4 tsp peanut oil
2 garlic cloves, peeled and crushed
1 red chili, seeded and chopped
★1 tsp dried shrimp paste
grated rind of 2 lemons
1 large ripe tomato, skinned, seeded and
chopped
500 ml/18 fl oz stock
★300 ml/10 fl oz coconut milk
3 tsp peanut butter
2 tsp salt
squeeze of lemon juice (optional)

Use a variety of vegetables for this dish,
e.g. green beans, cabbage, cauliflower,
broccoli, courgettes, pumpkin, bamboo
shoots, etc.

Prepare the vegetables: cut the
cauliflower and broccoli into florets, the
green beans into small pieces, the cabbage
into strips, the courgettes into slices, the
pumpkin into cubes and the bamboo
shoots into thin slices.

Place the chopped onion in a saucepan
and fry in the oil until golden. Add the
garlic, chili and shrimp paste. Stir and
mash the paste with a spoon. Add the
lemon rind and chopped tomato. Stir well
and cook until a purée is obtained.

In a large saucepan, bring the stock and
coconut milk to the boil. Add the
vegetables one by one, depending on their
respective cooking times. Cook until only
just tender but still whole. Stir in the sauce
and season. Add a little lemon juice,
if desired.

RUMP STEAK JAVANESE-STYLE

Serves 4

500 g/1 lb 2 oz rump steak, in slices
1 onion, peeled and chopped
4 garlic cloves, peeled and crushed
3 tbsp thick soya sauce
4 tsp brown sugar
1 tsp ground black pepper
4 tsp peanut oil
2 ripe tomatoes, skinned, seeded and finely
chopped

Place the meat on a chopping board and
flatten with a rolling pin. Place the
chopped onion, garlic, soya sauce, sugar
and pepper in a liquidizer and blend to a
purée. Coat the meat with this mixture

and leave to marinate for at least 1 hour
at room temperature, or longer
if refrigerated.

Drain the meat from the marinade.
Reserve the marinade and sauté the meat
briefly in hot oil over a high heat until
golden on both sides. Place in a
flameproof casserole, add the marinade and
the chopped tomatoes. Cover and cook
for 12 minutes over a moderate heat,
stirring occasionally, until the meat is
tender and the sauce is smooth and thick.
Serve hot.

INDONESIAN FRUIT SALAD

Serves 6

1 grapefruit
1 orange
2 apples
1 cucumber
1 small pineapple
★½ tsp dried shrimp paste
★½ tsp sambal-ulek
2 tsp brown sugar
2 tsp thick soya sauce
4 tsp lemon juice

Peel the grapefruit and orange, removing
all the white pith. Cut into segments over
a bowl to collect the juices. Remove the
pips. Peel the apples and cut into thin
slices. Peel the cucumber and slice thinly.
Slice the pineapple, peel and core then
chop into cubes. Wrap the shrimp paste in
aluminium foil and grill for 5 minutes,
turning so that both sides are done. Mix
the shrimp paste, sambal-ulek and sugar
with the soya sauce and lemon juice. Pour
the sauce over the fruit and mix. Leave to
stand for several minutes before serving.

Top: Vegetables with Coconut Sauce
Bottom: Rump Steak Javanese-style

PINEAPPLE WITH COCONUT

Serves 6

1 small, slightly underripe pineapple
2 tsp oil
1 small onion, peeled and finely chopped
1 garlic clove, finely chopped
1 small stick cinnamon
3 cardamom pods
3 cloves
3 tsp ground coriander
1½ tsp ground cumin
1 red chili, seeded and chopped
1 tsp salt
★225 ml/8 fl oz coconut cream
1 tsp brown sugar

Slice the pineapple, peel and core, then cut into cubes.

Heat the oil in a frying-pan and sauté the chopped onion with the garlic, cinnamon, cardamom and cloves over a very high heat, stirring occasionally. When the onion is soft, add the coriander, cumin, chili and salt. Stir and fry for a few more seconds until the spices turn a dark brown colour. Add the pineapple cubes and coat in the mixture. Add the coconut cream and sugar then bring to the boil, stirring constantly. Simmer for 3-4 minutes, uncovered, until the pineapple is tender, but not too soft.

RICE FLAVOURED WITH COCONUT MILK

Serves 6

500 g/1 lb 2 oz long-grain rice
★1 litre/1¾ pints coconut milk
1 tsp salt
1 onion, peeled and finely chopped
2 garlic cloves, finely chopped
1 tsp ground turmeric
1 tsp ground cumin
1 tsp ground coriander
★½ tsp dried shrimp paste
1 tsp grated lemon rind

Wash the rice and drain well. Place the remaining ingredients in a saucepan, bring to the boil, stirring frequently, then add the rice. Stir well and when the mixture comes to the boil again, cover and leave to cook over a low heat for 20 minutes. Uncover and gently stir the rice with a fork to help it absorb the coconut milk. Cover again and leave to cook for a further 5 minutes. Serve hot as an accompaniment.

**Below left: Pineapple with Coconut
Below right: Aubergines with
Yoghurt (recipe on page 25)
Opposite top: Rice Flavoured with
Coconut Milk
Opposite bottom: Indonesian White
Rice**

INDONESIAN WHITE RICE

Serves 6

500 g/1 lb 2 oz short or round-grain rice
750 ml/1¾ pints water
2 tsp salt

Place the rice, water and salt in a saucepan and bring to the boil. Cover tightly and simmer for 15 minutes. The rice will be cooked perfectly if the pan is covered as soon as the water begins to boil. If you require softer rice, but without the grains sticking, use 100 ml/3½ fl oz more water. The rice should never be stirred during cooking.

GRILLED LAMB MADURA-STYLE

Serves 4

500 g/1 lb 2 oz boned leg of lamb, cubed
1 small onion, peeled and grated
2 garlic cloves, peeled and crushed
½ tsp salt
2 red chilis, seeded and chopped
*½ tsp dried shrimp paste
2 tsp liquid tamarind
2 tsp thick soya sauce
4 tsp grated coconut

Place the meat in a shallow dish. Mix the grated onion with the remaining ingredients (if you use dried, desiccated coconut you must add a little hot water to it first). Coat the meat in this mixture, cover and leave to marinate for 2 hours at room temperature or longer, if refrigerated.

   Push the pieces of meat on to skewers and grill, turning frequently to prevent the coconut from burning. Serve with rice and an appropriate sauce.

EGGS WITH CHILIS

Serves 6

3 hard-boiled eggs, peeled and halved
2 tbsp peanut oil
1 onion, peeled and chopped
1 garlic clove, crushed
*¹/₂ tsp dried shrimp paste
★3 tsp sambal-ulek
¹/₂ tsp ground galingale
★3 candlenuts, grated
¹/₂ tsp salt
2 tsp brown sugar
★100 ml/3¹/₂ fl oz coconut milk
2 tsp lemon juice

Arrange the eggs, cut side down, on a
serving dish.
   Heat the oil in a saucepan and sauté the
chopped onion and garlic until golden.
Add the shrimp paste, sambal-ulek,
galingale and grated nuts. Sauté this
mixture for a few seconds, mashing the
shrimp paste with a spoon. Then add the
salt, sugar, coconut milk and lemon juice.
Simmer and stir until the sauce thickens
and becomes oily. Pour the hot sauce over
the eggs and serve hot or warm. Only one
half-egg is usually served per person, since
this is a very hot dish.

NB: The sambal-ulek may be replaced by
the same amount of ground chili powder.
The candlenuts may be replaced by Brazil
nuts.

Eggs with Chilis

MALAYSIA

Malaysia is a green, exotic country, in the monsoon area familiar to readers of adventure stories. The exotic produce and the many different styles of cooking in Malaysia which evolved with the influence of the Chinese, Japanese, Hindus, Malays and Singhalese offer such a variety of dishes that it is a gastronomic paradise for any traveller.

The majority of Malays are Muslims and eat many fish, poultry and vegetable dishes. Pork is, however, deemed impure by Islam, although it is the main meat source in China. Hindus do not eat beef, since they believe cows are sacred. Nevertheless, the traveller is not restricted by these religious beliefs and so may eat everything.

As in all south-east Asian countries. rice is the basic food of Malaysia and is served at all meals. There is a wide variety of fish dishes, there are some unusual vegetables, and poultry is frequently eaten by certain creeds. The pork dishes are good and the sweets and pastries are very interesting, although fruit will often be eaten in preference to sweets - fruits that are through of as very exotic by western standards, such as the pomelo (related to the grapefruit), mangoes, durian (an acquired taste), rambutan, mangosteen and many others.

MALAY RICE

Serves 6

700 g/1¹/₂ lb halibut fillets, skinned
1 onion, peeled and chopped
4 cloves
60 g/2 oz butter
2 tsp flour
*2 tsp curry powder
*4 tsp chutney, chopped
3 pineapple rings, chopped
225 ml/8 fl oz milk
170 g/6 oz cooked rice
1 tsp salt
¹/₂ tsp ground black pepper
juice of ¹/₂ lemon
2 hard-boiled eggs, peeled and quartered

Remove any bones from the fish fillets. Place in a frying-pan, pour in just enough salted water to cover and add the chopped onion and cloves. Cover and simmer for

10 minutes or until just cooked. Remove the fish and set aside. Strain the cooking liquid and reserve. Melt half the butter in a saucepan, add the flour and curry powder and stir well. Gradually stir in the reserved cooking juices and bring to the boil. Simmer for 5 minutes until creamy. Add the chutney and pineapple, stir well and cook for 2 minutes. Gradually add the milk and continue simmering.

Meanwhile, cut the fish into bite-sized pieces. Add to the sauce with the cooked rice and season with salt and pepper. Sprinkle with lemon juice and add the remaining butter, cut into pieces. Garnish with the quartered hard-boiled eggs.

FISH WITH COCONUT

Serves 4

500 g/1 lb 2 oz fish fillets (e.g. cod or plaice)
90 g/3 oz desiccated coconut
170 ml/6 fl oz hot water
1 garlic clove, peeled
1 x 10 cm/4 inch piece ginger root, peeled
1 tsp ground cumin
*1 tsp garam masala
1 tsp salt
1 tbsp lemon juice
1 tbsp chopped coriander leaves
plantain leaves (optional) (available at West Indian shops or markets)

Cut the fish fillets into pieces 10 cm/4 inches long. Place the coconut, hot water, garlic, ginger, cumin and garam masala in a liquidizer and blend to a paste. Add the lemon juice and the coriander leaves. Place each piece of fish on a piece of plantain leaf or, if unavailable, on a square of aluminium foil. Cover each piece with 1-2 tablespoons of the blended mixture. Roll up the fillets, wrap in the leaf or foil and steam for 15 minutes. Serve hot.

TAPIOCA PUDDING

Serves 4

170 g/6 oz tapioca
1 small stick cinnamon
500 ml/18 fl oz water
150 g/5 oz palm sugar, chopped
*225 ml/8 fl oz coconut cream

pinch of salt

To be served with the dish:
225 ml/8 fl oz palm sugar syrup
225 ml/8 fl oz coconut cream

Place the tapioca in a saucepan with the cinnamon. Pour on the water, bring to the boil, cover and simmer until thick and transparent.

Place the chopped palm sugar in a saucepan and dissolve over a very low heat with 100 ml/3¹/₂ fl oz water. Add to the tapioca with the coconut cream and salt and cook, stirring constantly, until the mixture becomes very thick. Pour into a mould which has been chilled and then rinsed out with water beforehand, and chill until the pudding sets.

Turn out of the mould and serve with a bowl of palm sugar syrup and a bowl of coconut cream with a pinch of salt added.

Top: Fish with Coconut
Bottom: Malay Rice

YELLOW GLUTINOUS RICE

Serves 6

500 g/1 lb 2 oz short-grain rice
500 ml/18 fl oz water
2 tsp salt
1 garlic clove, crushed
21 tsp ground turmeric
1/2 tsp ground black pepper
*1 daun pandan leaf
*500 ml/18 fl oz hot coconut milk
1 small onion, peeled, thinly sliced and fried

Wash the rice and place in a saucepan with the water, salt, pepper, turmeric, garlic and daun pandan leaf. Bring to the boil, cover and leave to cook for 10 minutes over a low heat.

Add the hot coconut milk and stir well. Cover and cook for a further 10 minutes. Place the rice in a heated serving dish, sprinkle over the fried onion and serve.

MALAY SWEET AND SOUR PORK

Serves 6

2 tbsp flour
1 tsp salt
2 tsp sugar
*100 ml/3 1/2 fl oz water or buttermilk
700 g/1 1/2 lb pork loin, cubed
120 g/4 oz pork fat or lard
2 tsp soya sauce
4 tsp vinegar
120 g/4 oz pickled vegetables

Make a thick batter: place the flour in a mixing bowl and stir in the salt, sugar and half the water or buttermilk. Coat the cubes of pork with this mixture. Heat the pork fat or lard in a large frying-pan and, using a large slotted spoon, lower the pork pieces into the hot fat and fry briefly. Drain and set aside. Mix the soya sauce, vinegar and remaining water or buttermilk and sugar into the batter mixture. Place in a large saucepan and cook over a low heat for 10 minutes. Add the pieces of meat and cook for a few more minutes until the meat is tender.

Serve garnished with the pickled vegetables.

CHICKEN CURRY WITH BAMBOO SHOOTS

Serves 6

3 tbsp peanut oil
2 onions, peeled and chopped
2 tsp ground coriander
*1 tsp dried shrimp paste
1 tsp ground galingale
1 tsp cayenne
2 tsp salt
1 x 1.5 kg/3 1/4 lb chicken, jointed
*500 ml/18 fl oz coconut milk
1 can bamboo shoots, drained and sliced
*225 ml/8 fl oz coconut cream

Heat the oil in a flameproof casserole. Add the onions and sauté over a moderate heat for 2 minutes. Add the coriander, shrimp paste, galingale, cayenne and salt, stirring until golden. Add the chicken pieces and coat them in the spice mixture. Stir in the coconut milk, cover and simmer for 20-30 minutes.

Add the bamboo shoots, mix and cook for a further 20 minutes until the chicken is tender. Add the coconut cream and simmer for 5 minutes, stirring constantly. Taste and adjust the seasoning. When the oil comes to the surface, the curry is ready. Serve with rice and condiments.

SOUP WITH CHICKEN BALLS

Serves 6

350 g/12 oz chicken, minced
4 small onions, peeled and chopped
2 tsp grated ginger root
1/2 tsp cayenne
1 egg, beaten
1 tsp salt
1.5 litres/2 1/2 pints hot chicken stock
3 sprigs parsley, finely chopped

Place the minced chicken in a mixing bowl with the chopped onions and ginger and mix together, using the hands. Add the cayenne, egg and salt and knead well together.

Form the mixture into small 1 cm/1/2 inch balls and poach briefly in the hot stock. Remove them from the stock as they rise to the surface and season with salt. Strain the stock to make it clear, then continue simmering and put the balls back in at the last moment, to reheat them. Pour the soup into a tureen and sprinkle with finely chopped parsley.

MALAY PRAWN SALAD

Serves 6

120 g/4 oz fresh coconut, sliced
500 ml/18 fl oz milk
500 g/1 lb 2 oz raw prawns
1 bay leaf
10 cloves
1 tsp sugar
4 tsp vegetable oil
8 shallots, peeled and sliced
2 garlic cloves, chopped
1 apple, peeled and thinly sliced
2 tsp soya sauce
1 green chili, seeded and chopped
salt to taste
1/2 tsp ground black pepper
3 tbsp chopped peanuts
2 lettuce hearts, quartered

Place the coconut slices in a saucepan with the milk, bring to the boil and simmer for 30 minutes. Strain the coconut through a cloth and wring to extract the juices. Set the liquid aside.

Simmer the prawns in boiling, salted water with the bay leaf, cloves and sugar for 5 minutes. Remove from the heat and leave to cool for 10 minutes. Shell the prawns carefully and cut in half lengthways. Keep refrigerated.

Meanwhile, make the sauce: heat the oil in a frying-pan and sauté the shallots and garlic until softened. Remove from the heat, add the apple slices, soya sauce, chili, salt and pepper. Stir in the chopped peanuts and strained coconut cooking liquid to make a creamy sauce. Finally, add the halved prawns and mix well. Turn into a serving bowl and garnish with the lettuce hearts and fresh fruit, if desired.

Top: Soup with Chicken Balls
Bottom: Yellow Glutinous Rice

SQUID SAMBAL

Serves 4

500 g / 1 lb 2 oz small squid
2 tbsp peanut oil
2 onions, peeled and chopped
2 garlic cloves, crushed
*¹/₂ tsp dried shrimp paste
grated rind of 2 lemons
5 red chilis, seeded
★2 tbsp tamarind liquid
2 tsp brown sugar
1 tsp paprika

Prepare the squid: pull the head and
tentacles away from the body. Pull off and
discard the speckled skin and the ink sac.
Slice the body into rings and the tentacles
into strips. Place half the oil in a liquidizer
with the chopped onions, garlic, shrimp
paste, lemon rind and chilis and blend to
a paste.

   Heat the remaining oil in a frying-pan
and sauté the paste over a moderate heat
until it turns a dark golden colour and
separates from the oil. Add the squid,
tamarind liquid, sugar and paprika.
Simmer, uncovered, stirring occasionally,
for about 20 minutes, until the squid is
tender and the sauce has become thick and
oily. Serve with rice.

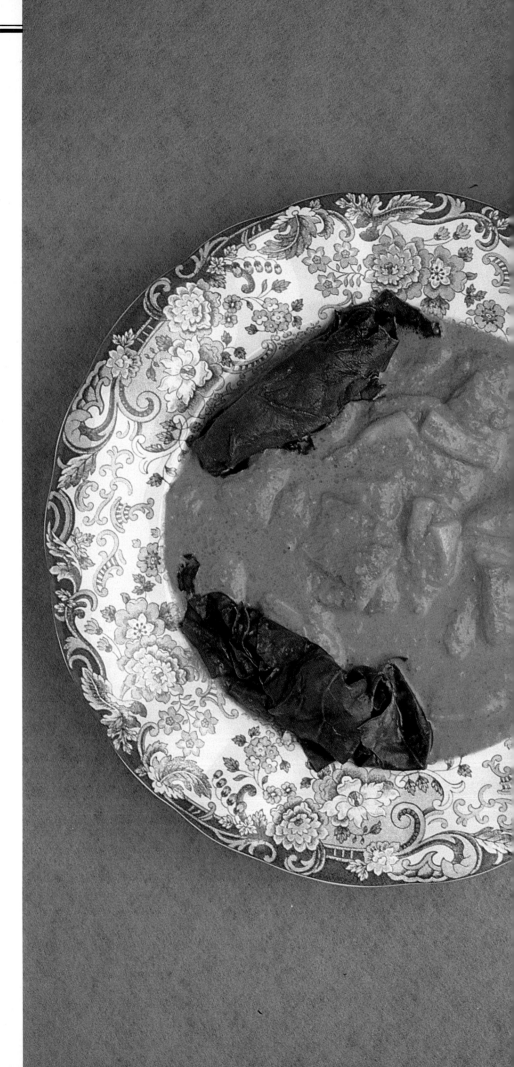

Left: Squid Sambal
Right: Malay Prawn Salad

RICE WITH KING PRAWNS

Serves 6

4 tbsp coconut oil
2 small onions, peeled and chopped
500 g/1 lb 2 oz rice
★1.25 litres/2 pints coconut milk
225 g/8 oz shelled peas
500 g/1 lb 2 oz raw king prawns, peeled
★1 tsp dried shrimp paste

Spice mix:
2 garlic cloves, chopped
small piece of ginger root, peeled and chopped
1 tsp ground coriander
1 tsp cumin
1 tsp turmeric
1 tsp cayenne

Combine the spices for the spice mix.
Wash the rice and drain thoroughly.
Heat half the coconut oil in a large
saucepan over a moderate heat and sauté
the chopped onions until golden. Add the
rice and toss until it takes on some colour.
Add half the spice mix and sauté briefly.
Add half the coconut milk and salt, stir
well then cover and bring to the boil.
Reduce the heat and cook until all the
liquid has been absorbed and the rice
begins to stick to the base of the pan.
Remove from the heat, stir once, and
set aside.

Meanwhile, cook the peas briefly in
boiling salted water, then drain well. Heat
the remaining coconut oil over a high heat
and sauté the prawns until they change
colour. Add the peas, shrimp paste and
remaining spice mix and stir well. Cook
for 2 minutes then add the remaining
coconut milk. Taste and adjust the
seasoning then simmer, uncovered, until
the liquid has evaporated. Serve the rice
with the prawns on top.

BEEF WITH PEPPERS

Serves 4

100 g/3¹/₂ oz butter
170 g/6 oz red peppers, seeded and chopped
90 g/3 oz flaked almonds
3 onions, peeled and chopped
10 cloves garlic, peeled and thinly sliced
grated rind of ¹/₂ lemon
salt and pepper
★500 ml/18 fl oz buttermilk
4 slices rump steak
3 tbsp oil

Top: Rice with King Prawns
Bottom: Beef Satay

To make the sauce: melt the butter in a
saucepan and sauté the chopped peppers,
almonds, two-thirds of the onion and all
the garlic and lemon rind. Season with salt
and pepper and add the buttermilk. Cook
over a low heat until a thick sauce
is obtained.

Cut the rump steak into thin strips. Heat
the oil in a frying-pan and sauté the beef
and remaining onion, stirring constantly
for 3 minutes. Add to the sauce and heat
through without cooking. Serve with a
lettuce or tomato salad and creamed
potatoes.

BEEF SATAY

Serves 6

500 g/1 lb 2 oz beef sirloin
1 tsp salt
4 tsp brown sugar
1 large onion, peeled and grated
4 garlic cloves, finely chopped
150 g/5 oz ginger root, grated
1 tsp turmeric
2 tsp cumin
1 tsp lemon juice
45 g/1½ oz peanuts, ground

For the sauce:
90 g/3 oz chopped peanuts
1 tbsp brown sugar
2 tsp grated tamarind
4 tsp coconut oil
1 medium onion, peeled and chopped
4 spring onions, chopped
1 small chili, seeded and chopped
*1 tsp dried shrimp paste
1 tsp salt
extra coconut oil, for brushing

For the meat: cut the beef into 2.5 cm/1 inch x 6.5 cm/2½ inch strips. Sprinkle with the salt and sugar and rub in well. Combine the remaining ingredients, mix with the meat and leave to stand for 20-30 minutes.

Meanwhile make the sauce: mix the chopped peanuts, sugar and the tamarind with 1-2 tbsp water. Heat the coconut oil in a frying-pan and sauté the chopped medium onion until soft. Add the spring onions, chili, shrimp paste and salt. Cook for 20 minutes or until the oil separates. Add the peanut mixture and 250 ml/9 fl oz water. Taste and add more salt if desired. Cook over a low heat for about 20 minutes until the sauce thickens.

Push the strips of meat on to skewers and cook over a barbecue or under a hot grill. When the meat is evenly cooked, brush with a mixture of two parts coconut oil and one part water. Lay the skewers of meat on a dish and serve with the sauce in a sauce boat.

Top: Beef with Peppers
Bottom: Chicken Curry with Bamboo Shoots (recipe on page 42)

BURMA

The staple food in Burmese cooking, as in all the countries of South-east Asia, is rice, served with many side dishes. The Burmese also eat a wide variety of delicious hot soups and a multitude of fish, meat and vegetable dishes. They do not eat desserts, since they prefer to serve fresh fruit. However, there are some sweet dishes which are eaten between meals and there are also refreshing, sweet beverages.

Although soups are served very hot, the other dishes are usually eaten at room temperature and are served together. There are numerous spicy condiments, as is usual for any country in this area of Asia, the favourite condiment among natives being 'balachaung'.

Although customs have been modernized and knives and forks are used, some Burmese dishes are still traditionally eaten with the hands, such as 'lethoke'. This dish is always served with a bowl of hot water and soap to wash the hands with afterwards

Often a Burmese meal will consist of one main dish, with numerous tasty side dishes and rice. Examples of these basic dishes that constitute a meal on their own are 'moh hin gha', 'Kaukswe' and 'htamin lethoque'. Once served, each person adds the condiments of their choice to these dishes.

FISH WITH SESAME SEEDS AND COCONUT

Serves 6

170 g/6 oz desiccated coconut
2 garlic cloves
2 tsp grated ginger root
100 ml/3¹/₂ fl oz hot water
4 tsp sesame seeds, toasted
2 tsp salt
1 tsp ground turmeric
1 tsp ground black pepper
juice of ¹/₂ lemon
4 tsp rice flour
2 tbsp chopped coriander leaves
1 kg/2¹/₄ lb white fish fillets

Place the coconut, garlic, ginger and hot water in a liquidizer and blend together. Pour into a mixing bowl and stir in the remaining ingredients, except the fish.

Cut the fish fillets into strips and lay on top of plantain or bamboo leaves, or rectangles of aluminium foil. Top each piece of fish with some coconut mixture, wrap well in the leaves or foil and steam for 15 minutes. Unwrap and sprinkle over extra toasted sesame seeds, to serve if desired.

BURMESE PORK CURRY

Serves 6

2 onions, peeled and chopped
10 garlic cloves
75 g/ 2¹/₂ oz ginger root, chopped
1 kg/2¹/₄ lb lean pork, cubed
1 tsp salt
2 tsp vinegar
1 tsp cayenne
100 ml/3¹/₂ fl oz peanut oil
2 tbsp sesame oil
¹/₂ tsp ground turmeric

Place the chopped onions, garlic and ginger in a liquidizer and blend to a purée. Place the purée in a sieve over a bowl and press to extract as much liquid as possible. Set aside the purée left in the sieve. Put the extracted liquid in a flameproof casserole and add the cubed pork, salt, vinegar, cayenne and half the peanut oil. Bring to the boil, cover and cook for 1-1 ¹/₂ hours over a low heat until the meat is tender.

Heat the remaining peanut oil with the sesame oil in a large saucepan. Add the reserved onion purée and the turmeric and stir over a low heat for 15 minutes until the mixture takes on a dark red colour and the oil separates. Add 2 tablespoons of water from time to time, and stir occasionally to prevent the sauce from sticking.

Add the pork mixture to the pan and continue cooking, stirring constantly, until the oil rises to the surface again and the liquid evaporates. Serve with white rice and other side dishes.

BURMESE SALAD

Serves 6

100 g/3¹/₂ oz onion, peeled and sliced in rings
250 g/9 oz cucumber
250 g/9 oz cabbage
2 tbsp soya sauce
*6 tsp dried shrimp powder
2 tbsp lemon juice
4 tsp seasoned oil (see page 51)
pinch of cayenne

Soak the onion in cold water for 20 minutes, then drain. Cut the cucumber into 4 cm/1¹/₂ inch slices and chop the cabbage.

Make the dressing in a salad bowl with the remaining ingredients, then add the cabbage, cucumber and onion. Mix well and chill before serving.

Top: Burmese Salad
Bottom: Fish with Sesame Seeds and Coconut

Burmese Stuffed Aubergines

SEASONED OIL

1/2 cup good quality oil
60 g/2 oz onions, peeled and sliced
2 garlic cloves, crushed
1 tsp turmeric

Heat the oil, onion, garlic and turmeric together over a low heat. Stir and cook until the onions are golden. Strain the oil and use as required.

BURMESE STUFFED AUBERGINES

Serves 6

12 baby aubergines, weighing 30-45 g/1-1 1/2 oz each

For the filling:
500 g/1 lb 2 oz cooked prawns
pinch of salt
3 garlic cloves, chopped
1/2 tsp turmeric
1/2 tsp ground black pepper
1/2 tsp cayenne

For the batter:
120 g/4 oz flour
5 tsp rice flour
3 tsp cornflour
1 egg, lightly beaten
2 tsp water
salt
pepper
oil for deep-frying

Cut off the stalk end of the aubergines and scoop out the centre using a teaspoon. The opening should be a little more than 1 cm/1/2 inch in diameter. Soak the aubergines in water for 15 minutes, then drain.

Sprinkle the prawns with a little salt, then rinse and drain on paper towels. Chop the prawns and mix with the remaining ingredients for the filling. Fill the aubergines with this mixture, through the hole in the top.

Sift the flour, rice flour and cornflour into a mixing bowl. Make a well in the centre and add the beaten egg, water and salt and pepper to taste. Mix to make a smooth batter. In a deep-fryer, heat the oil to 190° C/375° F, or until a cube of stale bread turns golden in 30 seconds. Dip the aubergines in the batter and fry until golden. Drain and serve hot.

BURMESE CHICKEN CURRY

Serves 4

1 x 1.5 kg/3 1/4 lb chicken
2 onions, peeled and roughly chopped
2 garlic cloves
1 tsp grated ginger root
grated rind of 2 lemons
2 tbsp oil
1 1/2 tsp salt
1 tsp ground turmeric
1/2 tsp cayenne
pinch of ground cardamom
4 tsp chopped coriander leaves

Joint the chicken then cut into small pieces suitable for a curry.

Place the chopped onion, garlic, ginger and lemon rind in a liquidizer and blend, adding a little of the oil to make the paste smoother.

Heat the remaining oil in a flameproof casserole dish and add the onion purée, salt, turmeric and cayenne. Sauté over a moderate heat, stirring well. If it is too thick, add a few drops of water and cook over a low heat until the liquid evaporates. The mixture should turn a dark red colour.

Add the chicken pieces, stirring constantly. Cover and cook for 30 minutes, stirring occasionally. Add the cardamom and chopped coriander leaves, stir well and cover the pan again. Heat for a few more seconds to allow the meat to absorb the flavours. Serve with rice and other dishes.

FRIED KING PRAWNS WITH BEAN SPROUTS

Serves 4

500 g/1 lb 2 oz raw king prawns, peeled
250 g/9 oz bean sprouts
1 onion, peeled and chopped
2 tsp oil
1/2 tsp salt
1/2 tsp ground black pepper
4 tsp soya sauce

Cut the prawns in half if they are very large. Wash the bean sprouts (if unavailable, chopped cabbage may be used instead). Sauté the chopped onion in the oil for a few minutes, then add the prawns and bean sprouts and sauté over a high heat for 3 minutes. Season with salt and pepper and add the soya sauce. Cover the pan, remove from the heat and serve immediately. If preferred, omit the soya sauce.

Top: Fried King Prawns with Bean Sprouts
Bottom: Coconut Rice

COCONUT RICE

Serves 6

500 g/1 lb 2 oz long-grain rice
★1.1 litres/2 pints coconut milk
2 1/2 tsp salt

Place the rice, coconut milk and salt in a large saucepan. Bring to the boil, then cover and simmer, without removing the lid or stirring, for 20 minutes. If after 20 minutes the rice has not absorbed all the coconut milk, stir gently with a fork around the edges of the pan. Cover again and cook for another 5–10 minutes. Serve hot with a Burmese curry, fried king prawns, sautéed pork and pickles.

GOLDEN RICE

Serves 2

170 g/6 oz long-grain rice
2 tsp oil
★500 ml/18 fl oz coconut milk
pinch of ground turmeric
pinch of salt
4 tsp sugar
170 g/6 oz fresh grated coconut
4 tsp sesame seeds, toasted

Wash and drain the rice.
   Heat the oil in a saucepan and sauté the rice for 3 minutes, stirring constantly. Add the coconut milk, turmeric, salt and sugar and bring to the boil. Simmer, uncovered, for 1–2 minutes to thicken the liquid, then cover and cook over a low heat for 15 minutes, until all the liquid is absorbed.
   Preheat the oven to 150° C/300° F, gas mark 2. Separate the rice grains slightly by stirring gently with a fork. Then add the grated coconut and turn the mixture into a greased ovenproof dish. Sprinkle with the sesame seeds and cook in the oven for 20 minutes. To serve, cut into diamond shapes and sprinkle with extra fresh grated coconut and lightly crushed, salted sesame seeds.

THAILAND

As in the other southeast Asian countries, Thailand's basic food is rice and rice is the basis of Thailand's economy.

The rice most often used in this country is polished, long-grain rice. It is usually washed several times and then cooked in the usual way, allowing the rice to absorb all the water. Another way of preparing rice in Thailand is to wash it, leave it to dry overnight and then steam it. This method prevents the grains of rice from sticking more effectively, but on the other hand, it should be eaten immediately after cooking, since it dries quickly. Glutinous rice is also used, especially for sweet dishes.

A Thai dish always consists of a plate of rice as the basis, served with a huge variety of other dishes. This is usually soup, some dishes with a sauce and many side dishes (prepared beforehand and served at room temperature since Thais do not eat hot food, apart from soup which is served hot). Although knives and forks are used in Thailand nowadays, food is also eaten with the hands. All the dishes are served together and everyone helps themself from the selection of dishes. Note that salt is never added to rice during cooking, since the sauces and seasonings served at the table have enough seasoning to add flavour to any dish.

COCONUT CREAM

Serves 8

⋆750 ml/1¼ pints coconut milk
150 g/5 oz sugar
6 eggs, lightly beaten

Preheat the oven to 180° C/350° F, gas mark 4. Heat the coconut milk in a saucepan, add the sugar and stir until it has completely dissolved. Add the beaten eggs, stirring constantly, then strain into 8 individual ramekins lined with greaseproof paper. Place the ramekins in a roasting tin half-filled with hot water and bake in the oven for about 50 minutes until the cream sets. Leave to cool then chill overnight. Turn out on to serving dishes and decorate with grated coconut and fresh fruit, if desired.

GREEN FISH CURRY

Serves 4

500 g/1 lb 2 oz fish fillets (e.g. cod or plaice), skinned
750 ml/1¼ pints coconut milk
⋆4 tsp green Thai curry paste
2 lemon tree leaves, if available
1 tsp salt
2 tsp fish sauce (see page 54)
2 small green chilis, seeded and chopped
2 basil leaves, chopped

Remove any bones from the fish and cut the fillets into slivers.

Place the coconut milk in a saucepan and bring to the boil. Add the curry paste, stirring constantly. Lower the heat and simmer, uncovered, for 10 minutes. Add

Coconut Cream

the slivers of fish and leave to cook for 15 minutes over a low heat. Add the lemon tree leaves, salt and fish sauce. After 2 minutes add the chopped chilis and basil leaves. Cook for a few more minutes then serve with white rice.

FISH SAUCE

3 tbsp oil
2 onions, peeled and chopped
4 ripe tomatoes, skinned, seeded and chopped
4 tsp vinegar
2 red chilis, seeded and chopped
salt and pepper
2 tbsp chopped coriander leaves

Heat the oil in a saucepan and sauté the chopped onions until golden. Add the chopped tomatoes, vinegar, chilis, and salt and pepper to taste. Cover and leave to cook for 20 minutes, without removing the lid, until the tomatoes have turned to purée and the sauce has thickened. Stir in the coriander just before serving.

SPICY CHICKEN

Serves 6

Marinade:
2 tbsp soya sauce
4 garlic cloves, chopped
1 tsp grated ginger root
1/2 tsp ground cinnamon
pinch of ground cloves
1 tsp ground coriander
1 tsp ground black pepper
pinch of crushed aniseed
pinch of cayenne

1 x 1 kg/2 1/4 lb chicken

Place all the marinade ingredients in a bowl and mix well together. Rub the marinade into the chicken and leave to stand at room temperature for 4-5 hours, turning occasionally in the marinade.

Preheat the oven to 200° C/400° F, gas mark 6. Place the chicken on a wire rack over a roasting tin and cook in the oven for about 1 hour until cooked through. Divide the chicken into 12 pieces and serve hot with rice and other side dishes.

GARLIC AND PEPPER CHICKEN

Serves 4

1 x 1.5 kg/3 1/4 lb chicken, jointed
4 tsp black peppercorns
6 garlic cloves
2 tsp salt
4 sprigs fresh coriander with the roots, chopped
4 tsp lemon juice

Cut the chicken joints into bite-size pieces. Crush the black peppercorns with a pestle and mortar and place in a mixing bowl. Crush the garlic in the same way and add to the peppercorns with the chopped coriander and lemon juice. Mix well together and rub into the chicken. Place the chicken pieces in a bowl, cover and leave to marinate for at least 1 hour at room temperature or overnight in the refrigerator.

Preheat the grill to medium and cook the chicken for about 20 minutes, turning every 5 minutes until the meat is tender and the skin is crunchy. This is an ideal dish to cook on a barbecue. Serve with white rice, chopped tomatoes sprinkled with a little cayenne, salt, lemon juice and thinly sliced onion.

STEAMED RICE

:Serves 6

500 g/1 lb 2 oz long-grain rice
750 ml/1 1/4 pints water

Place the rice and water in a saucepan and bring to the boil. Reduce the heat and simmer, uncovered, over a very low heat until the water evaporates and small dents form on the surface of the rice. Place the rice in a steamer and steam for 25-30 minutes. The grains should remain whole and separate.

THAI FRIED RICE

Serves 4

2 tbsp peanut oil
2 onions, peeled and chopped
1 large pork chop
250 g/9 oz raw peeled king prawns
200 g/7 oz crab meat
3 eggs
salt
pepper
700 g/1 1/2 lb cold steamed rice
4 tsp fish sauce
4 tsp tomato purée

120 g/4 oz spring onions, chopped
2 tbsp chopped coriander leaves

Heat the oil in a frying-pan and sauté the chopped onions over a moderate heat, until soft but not coloured, stirring occasionally. Meanwhile, cut the meat from the chop into small cubes. Add to the onions and sauté for 3 minutes over a high heat. Then add the prawns and crab meat and sauté for a further 3 minutes.

Beat the eggs and season with salt and pepper. Pour them into the middle of the pan and stir until they set. Add the rice and sauté, stirring constantly. Season with the fish sauce and mix well. Add the tomato purée and mix until the rice turns red (add a little cayenne if necessary).

Remove from the heat and add the chopped spring onions, Sprinkle with the coriander leaves and serve.

Top: Spicy Chicken
Bottom: Garlic and Pepper Chicken

PRAWNS WITH TOMATO

Serves 6

18 raw king prawns, peeled
salt
4 tsp cornflour
550 g/1¹/₄ lb cucumbers
60 g/2 oz lard
300 g/10 oz onions, peeled and sliced
550 g/1¹/₄ lb tomatoes, skinned, seeded and diced
225 ml/8 fl oz fish stock
2 tsp sugar
2 tbsp chopped parsley

Cut the prawns lengthways down the middle, without separating the 2 pieces. Open them and sprinkle with salt and cornflour. Cut the cucumbers into 5 cm/2 inch fingers.

Heat half the lard in a frying-pan and sauté the prawns until they colour. Remove and drain. Heat the remaining fat in the pan and sauté the onion and cucumber for 2 minutes over a moderate heat. Add the diced tomatoes and simmer until they soften. Pour over the stock and add the sugar and a little salt. Simmer for 20 minutes, then add the prawns and heat through. Arrange the prawns on a heated serving dish and garnish with chopped parsley. Serve with rice and other side dishes.

KING PRAWNS IN RED CURRY

Serves 4

500 g/1 lb 2 oz raw king prawns
★500 ml/15 fl oz coconut milk
★4 tsp red Thai curry paste
4 tsp Vietnamese fish sauce
1 red chili, seeded

Peel the king prawns, keeping the heads on.

Place the coconut milk in a saucepan with the curry paste, fish sauce and chili. Bring to the boil, stirring constantly, then add the prawns. Cook over a low heat for 15 minutes, continuing to stir. Remove the chili before serving. This dish is tastier if made the day before. Serve hot with rice and other dishes.

N.B. The heads should not be removed from the prawns since they give a wonderful flavour to the dish.

Left: Prawns with Tomato
Right: King Prawns in Red Curry

KING PRAWN SOUP WITH MEATBALLS

Serves 6

350 g/12 oz raw peeled king prawns
salt
250 g/9 oz lean pork, minced
2 tbsp finely chopped leeks
2 tsp grated ginger root
1 egg, beaten
2 carrots, peeled
2 litres/3¼ pints chicken stock
6 Chinese leaves, chopped
2 leeks, cut diagonally into 2.5 cm/1 inch
pieces

Rub the prawns with salt, then wash and drain them. Cut lengthways down the middle without separating the two pieces and sprinkle with salt.

Place the minced pork in a mixing bowl with the chopped leeks, ginger, beaten egg and salt to taste. Mix well together then roll into 1 cm/½ inch balls.

Make flower shapes from the carrots: cut 4 grooves along the length of each carrot, then slice the carrots thinly to achieve the shape. Parboil the carrot shapes, drain and set aside.

Bring the stock to the boil and add the meatballs. Then add the prawns and simmer for 5 minutes over a low heat. Add the chopped Chinese leaves, leeks and carrots. Cook for a few more minutes, taste and adjust the seasoning and serve.

FRIED RICE WITH PEPPERS

Serves 4

1 pork chop
2 tbsp peanut oil
1 large onion, peeled and chopped
1 red pepper, seeded and chopped
1 green pepper, seeded and chopped
1 tsp red Thai curry paste
500 g/1 lb 2 oz raw peeled king prawns,
finely chopped
700 g/1½ lb cold steamed rice
2 eggs, beaten
salt
2 tbsp Vietnamese fish sauce
170 g/6 oz spring onions, chopped (including stalks)
30 g/1 oz chopped coriander leaves

Remove the bone from the pork chop and cut the meat into cubes. Heat the oil in a frying-pan and sauté the chopped onion and peppers until softened. Add the curry paste and cook until the oil separates. Add the cubed pork and sauté until cooked. Add the prawns and cook, stirring, until they turn pink. Then add the rice and mix well with the curry. Season the beaten eggs with salt, make a space at the side of the frying-pan and add the eggs. Gradually mix in with the rest of the curry.

When the eggs are cooked, add the fish sauce. Stir and remove from the heat. Add the chopped spring onions and garnish with the coriander leaves.

SWEET PORK

Serves 4

500 g/1 lb 2 oz lean pork, thinly sliced
170 g/6 oz palm sugar or brown sugar
100 ml/3½ fl oz Vietnamese fish sauce
750 ml/1¼ pints water
60 g/2 oz fatty pork, cubed

Place all the ingredients in a flameproof casserole and bring to the boil. Cover and simmer for 30-40 minutes. Uncover and continue cooking the mixture until the meat is tender and the fat is transparent. Remove from the heat and allow the meat to cool without removing from the sauce.

This dish is usually served as an accompaniment but may also be served on its own, with white rice, vegetables and an appropriate sauce.

RED BEEF CURRY

Serves 6

★500 ml/18 fl oz coconut milk
2 tbsp red Thai curry paste
1 kg/2¼ lb stewing beef, diced
★500 ml/18 fl oz coconut cream
2 lemon tree leaves, if available
1 tsp salt
4 tsp fish sauce
2 red chilis, seeded and chopped

Heat the coconut milk in a flameproof casserole, stirring constantly, until it comes to the boil. Cover and simmer until the milk thickens and the oil begins to separate. Add the red curry paste and cook for 5 minutes, stirring constantly.

When the mixture gives off a strong aroma, add the meat and stir well. Add the remaining ingredients and bring to the boil, stirring constantly. Cook over a low heat for about 1 hour until the meat is tender and the sauce is reduced. Stir in a little more coconut milk or water if necessary. The sauce should be red, oily and rich. Serve with rice and other side dishes.

Top: Fried Rice with Peppers
Bottom: Sweet Pork

VIETNAM

As with all the previous south-east Asian countries, rice and a variety of soups form the basis of Vietnamese cuisine. Often soup, such as 'pho', made with ox-meat, is eaten as a main dish.

Rice is cooked without salt in the traditional way which allows the rice to absorb all the water. Grilled rice is a Vietnamese dish which is full of flavour. Chicken is one of the most popular dishes, although other types of poultry are eaten. Pork is the most commonly eaten red meat among the working class in Vietnam, since ox is a delicacy. Fish and seafood are also popular and form the basis of many delicious dishes.

The Vietnamese adore salads, some simple, others complicated. The more complicated ones incorporate aromatic plants, spices and very spicy sauces. Vegetable dishes are equally common in Vietnam. Fruit is eaten raw and most foods are steamed, making Vietnamese cuisine very light to eat.

SWEET PORK AND ONIONS

Serves 6

1.25 kg/2½ lb stewing pork
4 tsp oil
3 spring onions, finely chopped
2 tsp sugar
½ tsp salt
pinch of ground black pepper
850 ml/1½ pints water
4 tsp Vietnamese fish sauce

Cut the meat into large cubes, without removing the fat, since it adds more flavour. Heat the oil in a flameproof casserole and sauté the spring onions until golden. Add the pork and sauté until the meat loses its pink colour. Add the sugar, salt and pepper and continue to sauté until the meat is golden. Add the water and simmer, uncovered, for 1 hour. Stir in the fish sauce and continue cooking until the pieces of meat are almost dry. Once the liquid has been absorbed, stir constantly. Serve with white rice.

PORK CHOPS COOKED WITHOUT SAUCE

Serves 6

700 g/1½ lb lean pork chops
4 tsp hot water
4 tsp Vietnamese fish sauce
2 tsp sugar
3 spring onions, trimmed
½ tsp black pepper

Bone the chops and slice the meat thinly. Place the meat in a flameproof casserole, just large enough to take the meat in one layer, to avoid the small amount of liquid evaporating too quickly. Add the remaining ingredients and cook over a high heat for 2 minutes. Lower the heat and cook, uncovered, for a further 20 minutes or until the liquid has been completely absorbed. Stir occasionally to prevent the meat sticking. Serve with rice and green vegetables or with a salad.

CHICKEN AND PUMPKIN SOUP

Serves 6

¹/₂ chicken, weighing 500 g/1 lb 2 oz
1 kg/2¹/₄ lb pumpkin
6 spring onions, chopped
1.1 litres/2 pints water
1 tsp salt
2 tsp Vietnamese fish sauce
¹/₂ tsp ground black pepper

Cut the chicken into small pieces. Peel the pumpkin, remove the spongy part and the seeds in the middle. Chop the flesh into small pieces.

Place the chicken pieces, chopped spring onions, water and salt in a saucepan, cover and bring to the boil. Simmer for about 30 minutes until the liquid reduces a little. Add the pumpkin and cook for 1 minute only. Add the fish sauce and pepper and serve hot with rice.

N.B.: If pumpkin is unavailable, use squash or courgettes instead.

VIETNAMESE TOASTED RICE

350 g/12 oz long-grain rice
30 g/1 oz lard
450 ml/15 fl oz hot water

If the rice is powdery, wash it and leave to drain for 30 minutes, since it must be completely dry. Heat the lard in a frying-pan and sauté the rice, stirring constantly. After 10-15 minutes, the rice will go golden. Add the hot water, bring to the boil, then cover and leave to cook over very low heat for 20 minutes. This rice is served with many dishes.

GIA SAO' CHICKEN

Serves 6

1 x 1 kg/2¹/₄ lb chicken
2 tbsp oil
salt
pepper
2 tsp unsalted peanuts, toasted and chopped
1 red chili, seeded and sliced
4 tsp coarsely chopped parsley

Cut the chicken into large pieces. Heat the oil in a large frying-pan over a high heat and sauté the chicken pieces until golden and tender. Remove from the pan, drain and season with salt and pepper to taste. Arrange the chicken pieces on a serving dish and top with the chopped peanuts and chili slices. Garnish the edges with the chopped parsley (use flat-leafed parsley, if available).

Top: Chicken and Pumpkin Soup
Bottom: Vietnamese Toasted Rice

MARINATED FISH SALAD

Serves 4

500 g/1 lb 2 oz white fish fillets, skinned
120 ml/4 fl oz lemon juice
500 g/1 lb 2 oz runner beans, sliced
4 spring onions, finely chopped
2 garlic cloves, chopped
1 red chili, seeded and finely chopped
2 tsp Vietnamese fish sauce

To serve:
1 lettuce
1 bunch of mint
1 bunch of coriander

Remove any bones from the fish and flake the flesh. Place the fish in a non-metallic dish and sprinkle with the lemon juice. Mix well and leave to marinate for 3 hours at room temperature or overnight in the refrigerator.

Just before serving add the remaining ingredients to the fish. Separate the lettuce into leaves.

To serve, place a little of the mixture on a lettuce leaf, add a sprig of mint and 2 coriander leaves. To eat, fold the leaf into a parcel.

SQUID STUFFED WITH PORK

Serves 6

6 dried mushrooms, stalks removed
250 g/9 oz minced pork
90 g/3 oz transparent noodles
1 garlic clove, crushed
3 spring onions, chopped
1/2 tsp salt
1/2 tsp ground black pepper
2 tsp Vietnamese fish sauce
500 g/1 lb 2 oz squid
2-3 tbsp peanut oil
1 lettuce, shredded

Soak the dried mushrooms in hot water for 30 minutes. Drain and chop, then mix with the minced pork. Meanwhile, soak the transparent noodles in hot water for 20 minutes, then drain and chop coarsely. Add the noodles to the pork stuffing mixture. Stir in the garlic, spring onions, salt, pepper and fish sauce and mix well.

Prepare the squid: pull the head and tentacles away from the body. Pull off and discard the speckled skin and the ink sac. Cut off the tentacles, chop finely and add to the stuffing mixture. Stuff the squid, pushing the mixture well into the body, then close the opening by sewing it up with a needle and thread.

Heat the oil in a large frying-pan and sauté the squid for 5 minutes over a moderate heat. Thread the squid on to a fine skewer and leave to cook for a further 10 minutes over a moderate heat, or longer if the squid are very large and the stuffing is not yet cooked. When the squid are cooked, remove from the skewers, cut into thin slices and serve on a bed of shredded lettuce.

Left: Marinated Fish Salad
Right: Squid Stuffed with Pork

INDEX